Somewhere Out There
A Memoir

By Bert Arnold

"Somewhere Out There: A Memoir," by Bert Arnold. ISBN 978-1-62137-708-5 (Softcover) 978-1-62137-709-2 (eBook).

Published 2015 by Virtualbookworm.com Publishing Inc., P.O. Box 9949, College Station, TX 77842, US. ©2015, Bert Arnold. All rights reserved. No part of this publication may be reproduced, stored in a retrieval system, or transmitted in any form or by any means, electronic, mechanical, recording or otherwise, without the prior written permission of Bert Arnold.

Somewhere Out There

Introduction

IN SEVENTH GRADE I became interested in learning all I could about Greek mythology. The most important thing I learned was a maxim inscribed at the Temple of Apollo at Delphi: "KNOW THYSELF." That concept has intrigued me ever since. Years later, when I visited the Acropolis and sat in the seat of the oracles, I felt the wisdom of those words. I doubt if any of us will ever totally "know ourselves," but my life's ambition has been to learn as much as I could in order to be happy. To be happy was my parent's goal and neither of them attained their goal. I wanted to do it for them, but mostly, for me.

I wrote this book to convey what it was like to grow up in Bethany Orphans Home in Womelsdorf, Pa. during the Depression and World War II, and to describe how I overcame the effects of the traumas (abandonment, rejection, hurts, and other negative feelings) to achieve my goals in life. Memorable experiences, whether good or bad, become lasting memories, and they become our truth. When we attach emotion to them, we may not remember them accurately or we may misinterpret them. But by understanding them, one gains new insights. With the help of my family and friends, I have put together what I believe is a truthful account of my life. If I have offended anyone in this pursuit, that was not my intent and I am truly sorry.

For many years I felt my experiences were too intense for me to express in words whether they were joys or sorrows. Writing this book has been therapeutic and ultimately joyous not to mention challenging. I was forced to face my demons head on, and helped me to feel, reflect upon, and absorb much of what happened in my past. It reinforced my belief that happiness is an attainable goal, if we work hard at it. I have learned to bury some of my psychological pain, resolve other parts of it, express joy, sorrow, and live happily with myself.

Luck has also played a large part in my life. I was often at the right place at the right time, but more importantly, I knew it and utilized it to the fullest. I now accept my past and have moved beyond the traumas.

Despite my scars, my journey has been pretty successful. If this memoir affects you in any way, then I have enriched my life and I am grateful for the opportunity.

Thank you for traveling my road with me.

Bert Arnold
Upper Gwynedd, Pa.
March 1, 2015

Evan and I walking the beach where we could talk privately.

Chapter One

I WAS BORN TO Elsie Umbenhauer Gensemer in the Reading Hospital, in Reading, Pennsylvania, on Christmas Eve in 1930. My impoverished parents had four other children at home, with two more to follow after me. With little money and their marriage in shambles, chaos and a myriad of hurts and pain prevailed for all of us.

My mother with her seven children just before we were removed from her care.

I suspect my mother married my father because she desperately needed a home. At eighteen, she already had, an "illegitimate" child Ted, as they were called at that time, born to her out of wedlock which was considered a scandal and almost a sin in those days. Her parents and family had deserted her; leaving her lonely, depressed, and overwhelmed. The Pennsylvania Dutch have a custom called shunning and she was shunned. This meant she was put out of the family permanently with no home to go to or any way she could support herself. Her family never got in touch with her again. She married the first man who would have her who was my father but not Ted's. I don't know my father's role in the marriage, but perhaps he thought he loved her. Whether or not he did, it turned out to be a loveless union.

My mother found it difficult to give me a name, and I suspect it never entered her mind to think of one before my birth. She was too overwhelmed in her life to think about anything. My deceased sister was named Pearl because we lived at Franklin and Pearl Streets in Shillington, Pennsylvania. I wonder how Pearl felt about that or even if she knew. I was five days old when the doctor said she

The street sign near our house and where my sister's name came from.

couldn't take me home unless she named me. After he issued his ultimatum, the next person to enter the room was a woman named Bertha Rose whom my mother had never met. I became Bertha Rose Gensemer. That was name, not a very thoughtful name. My mother told me this story when I was in my thirties. The way she chose my name made me feel unloved. And haunted me for years. Eventually, I felt compelled to legally change it. I felt that if my mother cared about me, she would have picked something with a personal significance. Like most mothers, I myself had a name picked out for my daughter very early in my pregnancy. I still feel sensitive and angry if anyone calls me Bertha. I correct them immediately or I don't answer to it and sometimes I might state defensively and angrily, "That is not my name."

I have no idea how my mother managed my homecoming. I do know that when my youngest brother Carl was born, my mother walked five miles with him from Reading to our house in Shillington. That is unbelievable to me! We had no car and I don't know if there was any public transportation. Who knows if my father was at all involved with my birth—he never spoke about his children and may have been involved with his numerous girlfriends at the time. I can now empathize with my mother's situation, but she and my father were oblivious to the pain they inflicted on all of us.

My mother was 5'3" tall, overweight, and looked much older than her years. She was born in 1904 and had two sisters. Because she was deprived of a normal upbringing by her family and was an unloved child herself, she couldn't face any more pain. She was labeled the "black sheep" by her family at a young age and consequently lived her assigned role in spades.

She was too distraught about her family of origin to express feelings. I saw her show emotion on only one occasion, which I will describe in a later chapter. She was numbed from her many traumatic trials. In her defense, she lived without support most of her life. I don't believe she ever had friends and I know she never pursued help. No wonder she always looked bewildered, confused, and sad.

My father was a good looking man, 5'8" tall and 138 pounds. He was unable to be a responsible father, husband, or son. His childhood remains a mystery to me, as I never knew any of his family except his mother who never spoke about family issues, nor did I ask her, and I think she preferred it that way. She did visit us in the orphanage for a few years when I was quite young. I remember her as a caring woman who had little to say. Pennsylvania Dutch people don't talk about emotionally charged issues.

The Pennsylvania Dutch migrated to the states in the 17th and 18th centuries from southwest Germany and Switzerland. Our mother's ancestors came from Switzerland and my father's family came from Germany. My mother's ancestors came by boat through New York and settled in Berks County in Pennsylvania. My father's family arrived in Philadelphia and settled in Berks County from Pennsylvania Dutch countries. They speak a language called Pennsylvania German. My grandmother and mother could understand the language, but not speak it, so I never learned it.

My father worked sporadically and was emotionally unavailable. I have no idea what he did for a living, but I was told he was a janitor at one time. His major goal in life was to be happy, which he pursued relentlessly and unsuccessfully. He performed as a clown in restaurants for free as he was not a professional, and made beer for friends who were faithful only if he was passing it out for free. He was a womanizer. Most of all, he felt hopeless and overburdened. I learned all this from a letter sent to Bethany from the Children's Aid Society, which I was able to obtain and read only this year. Although he inflicted devastating damage on his wife and children, one good thing in his favor, was he never hurt anyone outside of the family. Like all of us, this says to me that he had a better side also. I have a need to believe that.

Our home was a former two-story drab dilapidated small factory that had been subdivided into three 10' by 30' homes. Each had two bedrooms upstairs and two rooms downstairs. We lived in the middle house which was windowless except in the back. Eventually our small home accommodated seven children and my parents, along with homeless girlfriends my father brought home from time to time. When I was an adult, I asked my mother how she felt about taking them in. Her response was, "What difference did it make? I couldn't do anything about it."

Our house in the middle section.

All the kids slept in one bedroom and our parents in the other. To fit us all into the bed, we slept heads to feet. Anyone else in the house slept downstairs, and I don't know what arrangements were made for them. During the day we all lived downstairs. It must have been miserable for them and us to pile into such close quarters.

On September 28, 1932, my 30-year-old distraught father visited his father at the Berks County Prison, where he was being held on larceny charges. He had "stolen public funds" while he was a clerk in the city sewage permit bureau. My father then walked a half block away and fatally shot himself in the head. He left a note to his father, requesting forgiveness but left us nothing except sorrow. A small insurance policy paid for his funeral, which I am told we all attended. According to his social worker, he was haunted by his inability to care for his children. He killed himself because he cared about us I want to believe. That is of some comfort.

My mother was now an overwhelmed emotionally dead woman, with neither the energy nor ability to care for her home and children. I have no memory of this time, as I was not quite three. Ted was her oldest child, age nine, followed by Sam, seven, Pearl, five, LeRoy, four, myself, almost three, Raymond, two, and five-month-old Carl. Neighbors complained when our mother sent us each day out into the streets so she wouldn't have to see or hear us until mealtime (turnips and potatoes almost every day) and bedtime. In this time frame, she would not have been accepted by neighbors. Pearl hated turnips and had to sit on the cellar steps if she didn't eat them. She remembered the huge cellar rats that scared her to death and later told me how painful this was for her.

The older boys were misbehaving at school, and the school reported our family to the Children's Aid Society. We were then given mental health tests to determine whether we were sane in order to be admitted to Bethany Orphans Home in Womelsdorf, Pennsylvania, about 14 miles west of Reading. They only accepted sane children because there were no children's facilities for the insane anywhere in the state.

The testing process justified removing us from our mother's care. She was labeled an "unfit mother." Ted, the oldest boy, was labeled "illegitimate," as was the norm for that era.

Eventually, six of us were admitted to Bethany. Ted was rejected because of his "illegitimate" status, being punished for our mother's misfortune. He disappeared from my life when I went into the orphanage. His father was alive but completely out of the picture, and I have no information as to who raised him or where. For most of my life I was ashamed about this birth. I think I learned from my fraternal grandmother about Ted when I was seven as, I had forgotten him and his plight. I do know that years later my mother told me she didn't raise him. He died in Reading several years ago, but I had never met him nor did I think of him as a brother.

Entrance to campus.

Our mother couldn't visit us for five years because of her designation as an "unfit" parent and the decision was made with no consideration of its impact on her children.

She didn't go with us when the minister drove us to Bethany. I still wonder how she felt to see us leave. Was she home when we were taken away? Did she say goodbye to us? Did she say she would miss us? Did she feel sad to see us go? These questions will never be answered, as all the involved people are dead.

I like to believe that we piled into the minister's car with no concerns, as I had never been in a car before and we didn't understand that we were leaving home permanently. He drove us directly to the Bethany infirmary, dropped us off, and left. No explanation was given to any of us as to what was happening. The infirmary was where all new admissions were housed for three days until the staff knew we were not infected with lice or other contagious diseases. All other orphanage patients were treated there as well. A wonderful doctor whose name fit him, Dr. Good, from Womelsdorf, came daily to monitor and treat all cases and to give us all annual physicals.

The infirmary itself was a lovely brick building with large windows everywhere. As all our residences were, it was immaculately clean. You could see two boys' cottages from the playroom, which was furnished in beautiful antique furniture and kept in excellent condition. The first floor had a patient room, a large playroom, an isolation room, and a kitchen. A 24/7 nurse supervised all services and lived on the premises. Upstairs were two dormitories with about twenty beds each, the nurse's room, and a bathroom connected to each dormitory, one for boys and one for girls.

Bethany Orphanage was a beautiful campus situated at the foot of South Mountain. It looked more like an elegant private school than an institution. A road encircled the perimeter of the campus. To the right as you entered were the church, the superintendent's home, and Moyer Cottage all surrounded by a beautiful mountain. Leinbach Cottage was to the right of these buildings. Going around the perimeter, to the right was the main building, which has since been razed. We called it the administration building. It had a large clock that chimed loudly every hour; as teenagers, it helped us know when to sneak home. You could hear it all over the town of Womelsdorf. If we heard it chime at five PM, we knew we were late. Did we hightail it back to the campus!

To the left of this long building was Santee Cottage connected to a large breezeway that housed the chapel. On the other side were the offices, boys' dormitories, a room for our principal, and two rooms for special education students, a program our principal started which was ahead of its time. To the left you could see farmland and the baby cottage, as well as the school for first through eighth grades and Sunday school. All the buildings were either stone or brick, quite beautiful, and well cared for. They were furnished with lovely antique furniture and designed to look as much as possible like homes. Professionals say that a well- kept residence is a healthy requirement for children and is how they learn to respect a home. It is hard for me to accept a messy home even now.

If you drew an imaginary line from the breezeway to the base of the campus, girls were housed to the right and the boys to the left. Rarely did we see each other, except in school or chapel. Even then we were not allowed to interact.

Flora and fauna abounded, as we had a full time gardener who planted flowers and trees all over the campus. Birds of many species such as Baltimore orioles, chickadees, and bluebirds were plentiful. A bus supplied us with transportation. Even, as a young child, the whole campus seemed enticing and beautiful.

A bakery was in the back of the campus, above the slaughterhouse. This was a lovely stone building also. Both play a part in my story. A road bisected Bethany from right to left; below it was a swampy dam where we swam or ice skated and a baseball field that I learned to hate. Directly above the dam was the infirmary, where we were kept for three days upon our arrival.

Chapter Two

I MUST HAVE IMMEDIATELY felt abandoned, as I spent my first day looking out the window and crying for my mother. Where was she? When would she come and take me home?

None of us were told why we were there or if we were going home. Not knowing was much harder than hearing the truth. This was another aspect of the Pennsylvania Dutch mentality: "Don't talk about it, just do it." I heard this said so often, I still often operate that way because it was so ingrained in me.

We played all day in a lovely large playroom windows on two sides of the room. I was too sad to enjoy all the available toys, so I began a survival technique that stayed with me for all of my years at Bethany. I looked out the window, waiting for my mother, and cried for three days. The pain must have been unbearable for all of us and some of it will never be fully resolved. It runs so deep that there seems no way to expel it.

Our infirmary. I spent hours looking out of the right window on the second floor. Girl's Dorm.

The nurse didn't smile very much, but she was a calm single woman who cared responsibly for all her patients. She never raised her voice and commanded much respect with her kind manner. Dr. Good, (the most fitting name for him) who came from Womelsdorf every day was a gentle caring person with a great sense of humor, so I connected to him quite early. Unfortunately, I didn't get to see him often enough to make a lasting connection. When I was older and an inpatient, he would give me a nickel for every bluebird I saw and counted outside the window. I still notice what birds are around me. At times I made as much as one dollar a day which I sent to my bank. No wonder I have always had a strong desire both at Bethany and in all my residences since, to have light and windows. Our condominium now has windows on three sides which are almost floor to ceiling.

At bedtime all six of us were taken upstairs to face our first separation. To the left was the dormitory for boys, so my sister Pearl and I went to the right. The nurse's room separated the dormitories. I wonder how my older siblings felt as we parted. It must have been a paralyzing jolt as although we were in the same dormitory, our beds were not necessarily next to each other, to encourage us to sleep rather than talk. I write this with a profound sadness and regret for all of us because it was not to be in our best interests. I was unable or didn't know how to express my sad and painful feelings except to cry quietly into my pillow.

Morning started with the nurse switching on the lights and bidding us a good morning. She said good morning to us and it lifted my spirits. After we dressed, we ate our breakfast on trays in the playroom. Two older girls from one of the cottages brought a stack of three food containers to the infirmary from the main kitchen in another building. The containers were round metal ones enclosed in a metal support. They fascinated me because they were so symmetrical and neatly put together. The girls served us hearty, mostly home grown food on trays in the playroom and returned the cleaned containers to the main kitchen.

After breakfast the doctor gave us physicals. In three days we got our health clearance and it was time to move to various cottages on the campus based on age and sex. None of us knew this was going to happen or what that move would entail. It was the beginning of some bad planning that would not occur today, but Bethany did the best they could and better than other institutions of that time.

Because of our ages, Pearl went to Leinbach Cottage while I went to Reed Cottage, and we remained separated for the rest of her time at Bethany. My two older brothers were placed in different cottages according to age, and were never to be in the same cottage during their entire time at Bethany. Raymond, age two, was placed with me in Reed Cottage, which we called the baby cottage. My youngest brother Carl, five months old, remained in the infirmary with the diagnosis of consumption, which now would be called pulmonary tuberculosis. He remained in the infirmary for three more months as a result of his illness.

Pearl was traumatized by her separation from me and was never able to accept it. Years later she told me she felt responsible for me before Bethany and felt worried about what happened to me. After all, I was her only sister. No one told her where I was or why we were separated. She felt lost and torn apart, and I wonder if this was the root of some of her future problems. But I'm getting ahead of myself and will come back to that later.

My siblings and I were never allowed visits with one another because separating us made life easier for the institution. Not once in all my fifteen and a half years at Bethany did they provide an opportunity for us to get together even when family was visiting. Boys were on one side of the campus and girls were on the other. Most of our activities took place in our respective cottages. When activities were a gender mixed group, staff supervised us to be sure we stayed separated. Now and then we caught glimpses of each other in chapel or the Santee dining room, but this was so infrequent that we eventually stopped looking for each other.

All cottages except Reed congregated for a worship service every night in the chapel. Boys sat on one side and girls on the other. When services were over, we marched out cottage by cottage. Occasionally one of my brothers would manage to be in the hallway before services (definitely illegal) and we would visit. This happened two or three times during our stay at Bethany. Why these visits were allowed I do not know, nor do I know what ended them.

Carl, the youngest boy, eventually joined Raymond and me at Reed Cottage but was immediately separated from us. He was kept in a playpen in the living room to prevent him from being contaminated by the other kids' infectious colds. When I turned five we were again separated; I stayed on the girls' side of campus and Raymond and Carl went to the boys' side. We were never to feel like a family again, even when we were adults. One of my brothers, LeRoy, and I are very close and have been all of our lives. He came to see me at Bethany after he left, and fed me many times when I was in college when both of us were broke. He loves having family around (especially his children) and has loved all of us unconditionally. He always said, "Just don't ask me for money. Go to Sam for that." My other surviving brother, Sam and I are not as close, but we do keep in touch when he comes to see me with his daughter or is willing to answer his phone. We also exchange holiday cards. My other three siblings have died, each from smoking. Fortunately, I never indulged.

Aside from Moyer Cottage, I liked the beauty of Reed the best. It was a lovely well designed brick building with a grassy terrace on either side of the cement front walkway. It had many windows on all sides. The first floor contained a kitchen, a dining room, a living room, a visitor's room, and a long playroom with windows along one whole side and glass doors. Through them we saw the playground and orchards. We could also see the farmers cut off the heads of the chickens we would eat for dinner and watch them run even after their heads were taken off. We thought that was so weird and we laughed as we watched them. There was also a dressing room, a bathroom housing, about six toilets and a tub, plus a staff toilet. Two dormitories were on either side of the bathroom. The matron's room was next to the dormitory where the youngest children slept. Upstairs was a room for the two older girls who were assigned to work at Reed.

Chapter Three

THE MATRON AT REED COTTAGE was a short, stocky, single woman about forty years old. She showed her authority in the way she walked and constantly snapped her fingers, which seemed to be a nervous habit. Her walk was too awkward to explain. This was pretty creepy to a three-year-old. And I don't remember her ever having a smile on her face. TLC (tender loving care) was never part of her makeup. She was organized and efficient but emotionally staid in managing her cottage of twenty-five deprived children, supervising a cook, and two older Bethany girls who assisted with chores and watched us in the playroom. Understanding or caring she was not.

Reed Cottage where Mr. Stoltzfus saw me in a self-directed play.

Years later I found out the reason the matron disliked me was because she lived near my mother in Reading and knew of her dubious reputation. As I got older, she would chide me about this with brutal frequency. "You'll be just like your mother," she'd say in a very disparaging way. Even at age three, I could hear the disgust in her voice. Obviously, she didn't like my mother, but I didn't understand why.

I swallowed what she said and complied with her rules to avoid conflict, which became part of my defense for years. Not today. I was very intimidated. Whatever I was told to do I did to the best of my ability, but inside I was dying. I was too afraid to not obey and I tuned out the rage that was building up inside me. If I rebelled I knew it would totally devastate me because the price was too high and there was no one to protect me if I was treated unfairly. I relied solely on myself, even at that tender age. If no one loved me, it had to be because I was unlovable, and so I soon learned to hate myself.

Punishment for infractions was to be sent to a big, dark closet with a large basket of dirty laundry in it. Unfortunately, I had my turn in there a few times and stayed until mealtime or bedtime whichever one came first. Only one child was in there at a time, and the aloneness made it scarier. I was so fearful of rats (even though there were none), that I would climb into the laundry basket and quietly cry. Crying was frowned upon and if you indulged around staff, you were shamed but you could let it out quietly in the closet.

No one cared about me or knew I existed. These feelings left me feeling empty like I was just a vacant doll. When I cried secretly, this is what I cried about. I was becoming a loner and developing a secret self. I would look out the window and yearn for my mother to come and take me home. I felt such deep desperation and panic. Although I was taken from her at an early age, I never forgot her. I saw her as a beauty and a kind person who loved me. Did she love me? Did she miss me?

Would she remember me? I didn't know. If she loved me, wouldn't she have kept me? What confusing questions for me to understand. Somehow, I still believed she would take me home when she could. I guess I was a born optimist.

Our routine was the same seven days a week, except that we had visitors on Saturday and Sunday. No wonder I can't stand routine now. It seems so boring and unproductive. I looked in vain for my mother each weekend when a visitor rang the doorbell but to no avail. I never got any family visitors nor any other visitors during the two years I was in Reed. Our minister sometimes brought other children to Bethany, but he never requested to see me nor my siblings. He did visit the matron because she wanted to visit. I longed to talk to him when I saw him, but again, to no avail. I believe he wasn't interested in us because he knew so much about our background. He just did his job and was not a people person. I got to know his son years later when we were both on Bethany's board and he was not a caring, sensitive person. I assume the apple didn't fall far from the tree in that case.

Our routine started at six a.m. when the older girls told us to get out of our cribs, which we slept in until we were age five. We were not allowed to exit our crib until the older girl put down the side. Regimentation became our routine. After using the facilities, we walked down a long hall to a dressing room. Our clothes were in a folded bundle and we were taught where our own clothes were so we knew which pile to go to each day; we picked them up from our assigned spots and then quietly dressed. An older girl grudgingly helped us if we needed help. I was living within myself and was mostly unaware of my brother, who was dressing in the same place as I was. I was seeing little of the environs around me. Any interactions would have been frowned upon, so when I did notice him I ignored him. I was so overwhelmed with loneliness at this time and I was staying totally within myself blocking out any unpleasantness. All I wanted was to have a mother's love and let me know they cared. I never stopped yearning for anyone to love me. That was never forthcoming. Once dressed we headed to a long playroom with a powder room, where one of the older girls washed our faces and hands. We lined up two by two near the door that led to the dining room. When we were all in place, we recited this jingle in a singsong manner:

Heels together
Hands behind your back
And stand up straight
And no talking at the table

Then we marched through the living room into the dining room to our assigned seats two by two making sure we stayed in the prescribed position the jingle dictated. It was compulsory to clean our plates and we did so because it was not acceptable to leave anything. I can't remember anyone ever challenging that rule and I doubt it would have been a safe thing to do. Not with this matron. Remember, this was the Depression, with 257 children on campus. It was hard to feed this many children, although we were never told that Bethany had a very tight food budget. I found this out when I became a member of their board years later.

When we finished eating, the older girl washed our hands and faces before we left the table. One washcloth was used on all of us without rinsing it between mouths. Horrible! Some kids had runny noses or food smeared on their faces. This made me cringe when it was my turn for the dirty washcloth. Ugh—I pulled in my lips and closed my mouth tight. If the girl had a bee in her bonnet, she pushed hard on your face. I had no recourse from this, but I can still remember the disgust I felt and the face I made. To this day I dislike food touching my lips so I constantly need a napkin close by. From there we were off to the playroom, where the older girls supervised us.

I dreaded that scary playroom. We behaved in the dining room, but acted out our feelings in the playroom. We were all angry kids, so we fought over toys or any small slight. I tried to avoid this by looking out the window and daydreaming about my wonderful mother who would come and take me to my lovely home. I imagined conversations with her, but she never came nor did she join in my conversations. Yet the fantasies provided some comfort from my sadness and solitude. I always imagined her caring for me.

There were six toilets in the bathroom and six kids were made to defecate at one time. That kind of regimentation is unimaginable to me today. There was no getting off the toilet until you did your job. In the meantime, the older girls made up our cribs. When we had finished our business, we chanted in a singsong manner, "Mary, Mary, I made a heapy." Then we would bend over with our hands on the floor while the older girls cleaned our bottoms. How humiliating, to say the least. Under those circumstances, I found it hard to do my business and I often was the last to get off the toilet. If you were there too long (as I usually was), you were chided to get going because," there are others who have to use the toilet." Like who can control the timing of a natural phenomenon!

One day I was looking out the window and saw a group of women looking in at us. One looked like my mother, and I cried out to her to come and get me. But when she entered the cottage I knew she wasn't my mother; she was Mrs. Bowman from United Church of Christ in Harrisburg, a supporter of Bethany. She told me years later that she was attracted to me because she liked my black hair and the fact that I was pretty. She had no children of her own, so she and her husband took an on and off interest in me during my years at Bethany and after I left Bethany. Years later, I realized I was important to them only if I was doing something they thought was impressive. While I was at Bethany they didn't think much of my accomplishments. I was just a cute little orphan to them. She always told me what to do when I saw her and I never trusted her judgement because she was so opinionated and dictatorial. The way the relationship worked out with the Bowmans, I should not ever have met them.

Christmas wasn't celebrated in Reed Cottage because we were isolated from the other cottages and we never saw evidence of celebrations. It would have been an extra burden on the houseparent, but since we didn't know any better we didn't know what we were missing.

One evening when I was four years old, I was asked to leave the cottage with one of the older girls. I was stunned. It was my routine bedtime, and I had no idea where she was taking me or why. She took me to a Christmas party in a large auditorium in one of the other cottages. The party was being given by the Bowmans' church and Bowmans requested my presence. But why didn't the Bowmans come to get me if they cared? Why was a messenger appointed?

The sight of all the Christmas decorations and presents was astounding. Why was I there alone? No one else my age was there. I was almost sick to my stomach from the excitement and more than a little confused. What was happening and who was I to answer to? I didn't have the vaguest idea. When we ate, Mr. Bowman sat on one side of me and Mrs. Bowman on the other. I felt imprisoned because I didn't know them. I withdrew into myself as I watched everyone doing their thing and kept my feelings to myself. Presents were distributed and mine went back to Reed with me. I was so unprepared for such a magical and overwhelming event. A part of me enjoyed it, but I couldn't express any joy. To whom would I have expressed it? I was put to bed when the affair was over and no one asked about the party, nor did I talk about it. I had no idea Christmas was an annual affair and I attended this party for three years before it was disbanded.

At age five I was very aware of our daily routine and had no reason to believe this wouldn't be my fate for the rest of my life. What a shock one summer day when I was packed up with no explanation or preparation. An older girl walked me halfway across the campus and dropped me off at Leinbach Cottage. I was told I would be staying there. Would I like it there? Who were the girls there? Where did I belong or did I belong? Why was I all alone without anyone to protect me and make me feel safe? Scary stuff to a small child. Who cared about me or my feelings?

It wasn't long before I realized the caring matron in charge of Leinbach did care, and especially about me. She became my guardian angel.

Chapter Four

MISS ANNA, THE MATRON in charge at Leinbach, was a kindly early 40's year old woman. She never seemed to be hassled and that added a sense of stability to me nor did she ever raise her voice at any of us. She wore housedresses with an apron over her dress which she took off only for church or days off. She even wore these dresses when she "dressed up" to go to her hometown or to Reading. She had no other clothes nor did she want anything fancier. She cared for twenty-five children ages five to eight with help from two older girls at mealtime. She was no beauty, but she had the soul of a saint. She took to me immediately and I learned to count on her for support and special attention.

Leinbach Cottage. Note seats in front where I learned to sew without a pattern and note the porches on either end of Leinbach.

Miss Anna saw my good qualities and encouraged me to utilize them by giving me more responsibilities than the other girls. She gave me opportunities the others didn't have, such as piano lessons or cleaning a teacher's room or taking the lead in plays. She was never obvious with words or emotions, but her actions spoke louder than words. I did not rebel or complain because I loved all these activities. Jobs gave me meaning and purpose, and still do.

When she was tired and had to get away from all of us, she took her bible and went to the woods alone to pray and renew herself. Sometimes she stayed there the whole day. I cried to go with her when I saw her go for the first time. She said she couldn't take me because she needed to rest from her responsibilities and pray and read her bible. She didn't go often, but when she did I never interfered again. The third grade teacher who lived at Leinbach took over for her. She was a stern teacher and when she was matron I feared getting on her wrong side. She put up with no wrongdoing. I waited impatiently for Miss Anna to return at dark.

Miss Anna and I after I turned 50.

Like all the cottages, it was a lovely two-storied home next to the woods. The antique furnishings left nothing to be desired and they were well cared for. All the cottages were kept in tiptop condition all the time. It looked like a family home because Bethany wanted the whole institution to feel like one big family. It never felt like family to me but on holidays, it did feel like a thriving happy community.

Leinbach Cottage had two beautiful big and long porches, one off the playroom and one on the other side with fancy antique rocking chairs, where we could sit in the evening and see the rest of the campus and perform quiet activities such as cards or puzzles. Miss Anna told us that whatever we did, it had to be done quietly because it was time to wind down. If we started to fight, Miss Anna would say, "Now girls stop the fighting." We would quit because she demanded such respect without much fuss from us. Then she would distract us by pointing out a lovely sunset or tree or whatever she thought would distract us from negativity. She was always willing to talk with us but it was understood that complaining wouldn't be heard.

There was a nice gazebo in the front of the building and that is where one of the girls taught me to sew clothes for myself. We sewed whole outfits by hand, as we had no access to sewing machines.

Our playroom afforded each of us a private locker. What a treasure that was to me! Privacy was a big deal and I basked in it. I kept secrets in there, such as money and mail I had received from Miss Anna's family or my maternal aunt's family. My money was allowance or gifts I got from extra chores I did. Rarely did staff intrude unless there was a problem. That locker became my personal home and my security.

We were assigned to one of the two dorms upstairs according to age. The younger ones were close to Miss Anna's bedroom. The teacher had a room next to the dormitories and we could smell her perfume coming through the door. I wanted so much to go in there and snoop, but it was locked and off limits. I became the assigned reader to the younger children which I did willing and I picked what I would read. Many times I almost put myself to sleep.

At six a.m. Miss Anna woke us up. We were responsible for dressing ourselves in the morning, making our beds (which became part of our routine for all the years I was at Bethany), and completing assigned chores without supervision. I loved working alone, in fact, I still do. We ate breakfast, and then each of us got a teaspoon of nasty tasting cod liver oil before going to our assigned chores. Miss Anna prayed with us before each meal:

Thank you for the world so sweet
Thank you for the food we eat
Thank you for the birds that sing
Thank you god for everything.

Miss Anna prayed with eyes closed and you could see her sincerity. I mouthed the words and only occasionally did I listen to what I was saying. She was one of the best true Christians I've ever known.

My first job was to clean two flights of steps and I can still hear Miss Anna saying in her soft gentle manner, "Get into those corners." My modus operandi was to do my jobs well to avoid conflict even when my unconscious rage was building up.

Once again, something new came into my life. I had not heard the word school. Now Miss Anna was telling me I moved to Leinbach because I was going to kindergarten in the fall. I had no idea if I would be happy or what it meant to go to school. During the summer we had recreation in the morning and boring tedious arts and crafts in the afternoon, so we could be kept busy all day and sleep well at night. Our crafts, plaster of Paris items or lanyards were sold on Anniversary Day. I thought they looked so ordinary and tacky; I got no pleasure out of making them. Of course, I didn't rebel. September and school seemed so far away.

The older girls bathed us two at a time twice a week. The girls would comment on our bodies and make disparaging remarks: "She won't be pretty" or "Doesn't she have ugly legs" or "She'll never get married because she's too fat." It was embarrassing enough to strip and the negative remarks added fuel to the fire. I wondered how they knew what I would be. I was scared and angry each time, fearing what they would say about me. Their remarks stung and stuck with me for a long time.

Any unsupervised play was a terrifying time, as there was a bully who tormented me endlessly. Her tireless taunting often produced tears when I was alone. I never told Miss Anna because she already knew how hard this bully was on me. Not much escaped her eyes. I remember when the bully told me I had a crazy sister who pulled out her hair. I had forgotten Pearl, as I hadn't seen her since she went to Leinbach Cottage before I was three. When I asked Miss Anna if it was true, her response was that I did have a nice sister in a special place and she was well and healthy. The "special place" Miss Anna referred to was the mental institution, Allentown State Hospital. Pearl had been placed there after having an acute psychotic break at around age seven. At that time there were no other placements or organizations for disturbed or psychotic children. She would stay there until she was eighteen, because Bethany was apprehensive about readmitting her in case her condition became chronic which it never did. Because I was the only other female sibling, I felt responsible for her breakdown. If only I had stayed with her, I could have helped her. I felt guilty about forgetting her too.

What made dinner delightfully eventful for me was my reluctance to eat. We couldn't control what was put on our plates, but we had to consume every bit just like all the cottages were required to do. I loved the punishment for disobeying which I did often. My dinner was carried to the kitchen and I had to sit at a table next to Miss Anna and the third grade teacher's table to finish my meal. I nibbled away at my dinner while I eavesdropped on their conversations. To please Miss Anna, I timed my rebellion to complete my meal when they did. By then it was almost bedtime. I had avoided the playroom for that night and avoided the bully as well. Any time the bullying got too bad for me to handle, I would sob and scream by the locked door until Miss Anna would appear. When she opened the door, I would cling tightly to her apron so she couldn't leave me. It was hard for her to pry me loose. I felt pathetically helpless and despairing at those times. I was sobbing and begging her in desperation to take me out of there. Usually she allowed me to leave and sent me to the dorm to read the bible. Other times she would make me stay so the bully and I would be forced to try to "work it out," which we never could. My life was hell and I was helpless to do anything about it. If I wanted to settle myself down, I would sit at the window and tell myself that somewhere out there things would be better. I would tell myself that my beautiful mother cared but was too busy to take me home just yet. After all, I was kept as busy as I imagined her to be. I desperately wanted her to come and take me away from my misery with no idea it would have been worse living with her.

 I was seven and my relief was indescribable when my older tormentor moved to Santee, the next cottage placement. Some of my desperation faded and I was able to be more relaxed but the emptiness and the psychological pain endured.

 My crying at night was an excuse for me to go to Miss Anna's bed to sleep. She would carry me into her big bed and keep me there until it was time to get up. There was no cuddling or kisses, but I didn't know enough to miss affection. Being emotionally deprived kept me unaware of these human needs. I have become a hugger and enjoy receiving them. I still feel unlovable at times and need to tell myself about all the people I know who love me.

Often Miss Anna would visit her lower middle class family in Bangor, Pennsylvania for the weekend and take me along. I loved the train and found it to be exhilarating and exciting. I didn't know what was expected of me in their home, so I followed Miss Anna around for clues of how to behave. I would play with her niece and nephew after I felt I had figured out proper behavior which relieved Miss Anna of her responsibilities for me for a while. I remember getting a box of candy each year from her family for Valentine's Day. That was so awesome to have a whole box of candy all to myself.

I had to sleep in a double bed with her. What a treat! The one negative was visiting her old bedridden shriveled up uncle, who scared me to death. She tried to convince me that it was safe to hug him, but I couldn't do it. Now I realize how much he would have liked that.

I loved mystery books, and Miss Anna was able to get my maternal aunt and my aunt's children to send me books for Christmas. I found out later that Miss Anna bought me the *Weekly Reader* out of her own pocket because she knew I wanted it. I wanted to learn about "the out there" that I craved. In her usual manner of not wanting to have favorites, she told me she didn't know who paid for it. She bought me a book about the missionaries Livingstone and I was mesmerized by their stories. They were American missionaries in Africa and I think she wanted me to become a missionary like them, but we never spoke about it. Miss Anna fit the Pennsylvania Dutch mold.

Chocolate covered thin mints were my favorite candy. I was enchanted with the neatness of them lined up in a box. She would make sure I always had them, even after I left her for the next cottage which was an unheard of phenomenon. She must have carried them to Santee while I was at school. Again, she bought them out of her own pocket but never admitted this. I was sure it was she because no one else knew they were my favorite.

Our treasurer, who was going to marry a Bethany alumnus, requested the most blonde girl and darkest brunette to act as flower girls. Miss Anna picked me as the brunette. I was so proud because we had our hair curled for the first time and were dressed up in new white dresses. I thought the marriage was all about me so I loved the whole affair. There was a ring in the wedding cake and I found it in my slice, which meant I would be the next to get married. I didn't believe I would be next, but I did think at least, it would happen when I was old enough.

I was chosen to take piano lessons. The music teacher constantly taunted me with negative remarks about my mother. She would say, "You will be like your mother." I feel this statement made me work even harder to accept the mantra that I would not be like her. Perhaps she resented the attention I got from Miss Anna. One day I got so angry with her taunting, I slapped her in the face and I was deprived of my piano lessons permanently. That behavior was not my usual behavior, but she was just too obnoxious for me to tolerate and I still think she deserved it. After all, at this time in my life, I loved my mother. Miss Anna never mentioned the incident to me nor did anyone else even though I know every staff member and teacher had heard about it. I suspect her personality left a lot to be desired for everyone. She never smiled nor did she exert herself to be pleasant. I have always regretted the punishment because I wanted to play piano.

Every Sunday until I graduated from high school, we had Sunday school in the morning, church in the afternoon, and chapel at night. How boring a day was that! We said prayers with every meal and prayers before bed. The fundamental teachings of the church made me feel as though God was watching my every move. One day as I was walking to school, I looked up and said, "God, you don't have to watch me every place I go because I promise to be good." I felt constantly judged by Him. He was just one more authority figure I didn't need. I didn't dare tell Miss Anna how I felt about God. She would have been aghast. I guess talking to him made me feel he heard me and I assumed he stopped watching me so carefully.

The third grade teacher left Bethany every weekend and requested one of us to clean her room for pay and Miss Anna assigned me the job. I was delighted because I could snoop and get away from the girls in the playroom. I read her diary and discovered that the teacher's only romance ended when her beau was killed in World War I; she was still pining for him and never did get married. I was sad for her, but it was a real treat for a seven year old to smell all her perfumes and powders. I earned $1 a week for a year and always banked it.

Bethany's Bausman Church

Miss Anna packed a suitcase for me one weekend and told me I was to go to the Roberts' house, an upper middle class family from the same Harrisburg church as the Bowmans. They were a childless couple who, unknown to me, wanted to adopt me. All I knew of them was they sent a two foot long chocolate egg to me every Easter that was full of Hershey kisses. I was quiet during the hour and a half ride to their house, which was well furnished and lovely. Most of the weekend I swung on their porch swing and continually vomited. I can't even remember what else we did. Was Bethany going to abandon me? After all, Bethany was now my home and I was very bonded to the institution and needed to go back to be sure I was not rejected. Again, I felt so empty. When the Roberts brought me back on Sunday, I was taken to the superintendent's office and told the purpose of the visit. I cried and said I wanted to stay at Bethany. The adoption was cancelled and I never regretted that decision. They never came to see me again nor did I ever get the Easter egg again. I still wonder how they felt about my rejection.

Sunday nights, Miss Anna loved to listen to the Moreland Sisters on the radio and we joined her. We huddled together in a small room around the radio. These were peaceful times with no fighting. What a pleasure! Little did I know one day I would sing on the radio just as they had done. We loved their singing and I still remember one of their commercial songs:

Oh we feed our doggie Thrivo,
They're very much alivo,
Full of pep and vim.
If you want a peppy pup,
You had better hurry up,
For its Thrivo for him.

I had no training nor was it explained why I was the one chosen to do the singing, but presumably it was because I could sing and I was known to be conscientious and would do a good job. I was driven to Reading by our treasurer. I felt I was a star like the Moreland Sisters. Bethany picked the song I was to sing and then someone would make a pitch for the orphanage. I was introduced on the air as a Bethany girl, but not by name, and I was never complimented for my performance. Raising money for Bethany was expected of us and compliments were never forthcoming about anything we did. Each Friday at school we had to write a letter to a parent or relative, so I wrote my mother telling her when I would sing.

For one Mother's Day, I informed her by letter that I was going to sing a song especially for her. Knowing she would tune in, I sang with great emotion.

You are a wonderful mother,
Dear old mother of mine.
You'll hold that spot
Down deep in my heart,
Until the stars no longer shine.

Years later she told me she never knew I sang on the radio and didn't hear my Mother's Day song. I was astounded because I had written her to listen each week, and especially on Mother's Day. It convinced me she didn't care about us and I felt crushed that she could be so callous. I see this differently now. She had to have been on overload all the time.

I was the appointed tour guide if church groups wanted a tour of Bethany. I enjoyed the compliment of being chosen, but the guests showed no interest in me and I wanted so much to be noticed. Again, I got neither thanks nor compliments, not even tips, although I was reliable and consistent. Maybe Bethany told them not to tip. Of course, I never complained, but I thought bad thoughts about the experience. These tours left me with feelings of nothingness as if I didn't exist and I felt disrespected.

Many nice excursions were planned for us. Every Saturday night, from first through twelfth grade, we went to movies on campus. I would immerse myself in the star's role and act it out in my head until bedtime, to avoid interacting with my peers. I would cry as I played back the sad parts while I walked back alone to our cottages. When I was in high school and relived these sad roles on the bus, I would cry quietly as I looked out of the window. I imagined me in those roles and stared out of the windows to hide my tears from the rest of the girls.

Miss Anna told us that we would take part in a state-run health experiment. We were not told who was conducting it or why. A placebo group and a control group would be put on a particular diet. I felt inferior to other people because my orphan status made me eligible and I felt used. They took our measurements each week and I can still hear someone saying to me, "Put your behind up against the blue board." It was a humiliating experience. The experiment was discontinued because most of us were too angry to conform to the rules.

I was ashamed for many years of being an orphan. I couldn't divulge this part of my life to anyone. I couldn't even tell my husband when we knew we were serious about each other. Instead, I told him he had to guess something terrible about me because I was too embarrassed to reveal Bethany to him. He made several wrong guesses. When he guessed I had been in jail, I was indignant and said, "No, I was in an orphanage." He burst out laughing because he couldn't have cared less. What a relief!

I was ashamed not to have a family. My understanding of family was that everyone was always happy and never fought. How much I wanted that kind of family and how naïve I was. Some of that shame still lingers with me today, but I'm working on it by studying my ancestors. I've found that my mother was the exception and not the rule for the Umbenhauer family.

Bethany took us to Shibe Park in Philadelphia for major league baseball games. I remember how sad I felt when Jackie Robinson walked onto the field and was booed. Every other player was cheered. I knew he was the first black to play on a major league team since the late 1800s, but I didn't realize his historical importance. I was shocked at the crowd's reaction because at this time in my life I knew no blacks. Bethany and Womelsdorf were lily white. If Robinson could qualify, why shouldn't he be accepted and cheered for playing? He walked onto the field so confidently that he set an excellent example for me. Because of Jackie, I learned to be more confident.

Once a year we were ecstatic about going by train to Hershey Park, where we were free to roam the park alone with $5 to spend. It was a magical day and I was on a real high all day. My clothes were new, my feelings of freedom were intense, and I took in every person, taste, and smell of the town and the park. Heaven couldn't be any better than that! The town smelled of sweet chocolate, which is no longer true because of regulations against pollution. I headed for Hershey's chocolate milk, as it was so rich and chocolaty. Today it doesn't have that same intense chocolaty flavor. When I ran out of money I told the operators of the rides I was from Bethany and got free extra rides. As we rode the train home to Bethany I would look out the window and daydream about my future life, where I could be as happy as I was in Hershey. In winter we attended two or three Hershey ice hockey games, but they were never as exciting as the park. We were never allowed to play sports except on the Bethany campus, so I never knew enough to follow or appreciate any sport. Football and soccer are still enigmas for me.

Margie was my best friend and kindred spirit. Her family lived in the town of Womelsdorf, so she was an "experienced" orphan and town girl. Experienced, because she got to meld with the town kids when she visited her family and would come back to Bethany with sex stories she had heard from the town girls. We never discussed sex with any of the other girls because virginity was a given among us, or so I thought. Margie's father let her date when she visited him and that made her the envy of the rest of us. We remained friends until her death. We were celebrating our 50th high school graduation anniversary and Margie was to come back from California and meet me. Instead, I went to her funeral in town that morning and attended the reunion that night with Fred, my husband. Years later, I still miss you, Margie. She taught me a lot about worldly things.

Miss Anna would take me to Reading every Christmas season to window shop and see the department store decorations and culminate the day with dinner in a Chinese restaurant. The day was exciting but the restaurant was the icing on the cake. I had never eaten Chinese food before and I loved the special attention and the food. I now take my grandchildren to Chinatown in Philadelphia every chance I get. Miss Anna's favorite was chop suey and I learned to like it. Now, it is probably my least favorite.

All the holidays were exciting and we were usually in a non-fighting mood on those days. The school held a big Halloween party with donated costumes and lots of decorations. My most exciting costume was Minnie Mouse when I was in kindergarten. I thought it was the most gorgeous costume and that I would someday be happy like her. I never wanted to take it off because I thought I looked just like her. My favorite activity was bobbing apples in huge tanks of water until I was sopping wet. Apples were plentiful all year round because of our two orchards. Today, I still love to make and eat applesauce.

The standard turkey Thanksgiving dinner was served in each cottage. Turkey was only served on Thanksgiving and Christmas, so it was very special. For both holidays we went to church before breakfast and chapel after dinner where the superintendent told holiday stories.

Christmas was way over the top, starting with Santa giving us a half-pound of clear toy candy a week before the holiday. The Sunday before Christmas we got a half-pound box of hard candies and an orange as we left church. On December 7, 1941, we were leaving church with the candy and orange when we were told about the attack on Pearl Harbor. I was a frightened 11-year-old, but only for a minute, as I was thinking about the marvelous taste of my orange. After all, Pearl Harbor was so far away but my orange was very present. I still eat many fruits and especially love oranges.

We would display our gifts on our beds and complain if we felt someone else got more than we did. We were most interested in each other's family gifts, because it meant that someone cared about us. My aunt and her children sent me mystery books, which I treasured, but those warm family thoughts faded quickly after the holiday was over.

Birthdays were not acknowledged by anyone. None of us were aware of each other's special day and neither did my mother or anyone else acknowledge mine. That hurt deeply after I learned about families celebrating them. We were so accustomed to no one mentioning our special day that I can't remember when or how I learned my birth date.

Good Friday was depressing. Miss Anna was quiet all day and would remind us to think about Jesus being crucified. I often tried to sleep during the three-hour services, but Miss Anna would tap me on the shoulder to listen. Our minister, the superintendent, would choke up as soon as he said, "And he gave up the ghost." Miss Anna would bend her head and freeze for a few moments, but for me these words meant that church was almost over. The story was so tragic I didn't want to hear it. I had enough of my own problems.

On Easter we had to attend church before breakfast. We couldn't look for Easter baskets until we were back from church. They were hidden outside of the cottage and some in the woods but only at the fringes. Chapel was held after a ham dinner. We were told to sing joyously because Christ was resurrected. I believed in Christianity somewhat until I was fourteen and began to question whether Jesus was actually perfect. I asked the superintendent, "If Jesus got angry with the money changers in the temple and turned over their tables, wasn't he imperfect? If so, how could he be called perfect?" He answered, "That is not to be questioned." Then he turned to my matron and said, "Take her back to the cottage and wash her mouth out with soap." The matron did so and we never spoke of it again. It aroused my doubts about Christianity even more, and, I told no one, from that time forward, that I was questioning the faith.

May Day was a charming outdoors celebration with singing and folk dancing, culminating with a maypole dance. When I was part of the dance I thought I was most important. We dressed in white, which made me feel like a princess. As usual, no one mentioned the good job any of us did—it was all done for Bethany. Clapping to reward performers? I knew nothing of that custom.

July 4th and Memorial Day featured picnics after ceremonies at the flagpole that reminded us why these days were celebrated. Taps were played in the usual manner to finalize the services. I wanted to weep when the echoes of the trumpets were heard and my thoughts strayed to the dead servicemen. This was so profound for me, maybe this set the stage for me to do volunteer work with Marine amputees during the Vietnam War. Hot dogs were served only during these two annual picnics, so they were very special to me.

Beginning at age six, we spent months preparing for Anniversary Day—the best day of the year for all of us. My high was like the one I felt each year at Hershey. These highs sustained me when the chips were down. I practically floated through the day and again we were left on our own which added to my ecstasy. It was a way to raise money for Bethany and commemorate the anniversary of the institution's founding. We carried hundreds of heavy place settings to three cottages, for serving dinner that day. I think this was too much for my young body, because my shoulders and wrists have always been weak. We scrubbed every building on the girls' side of the campus, including the walls and ceilings. We cleaned the church and chapel as well. A hired seamstress worked all summer on costumes for a religious pageant. We rehearsed all summer and I took part in it every year. Rewards were given for the best-behaved and most improved girl. I worked hard to win the most improved because it was a larger sum of money. One thing that got me the award was walking fast when I had to perform tasks anywhere on campus. The superintendent's wife liked all of us to hurry to our assigned jobs. Actually, I was usually fast because I was trying to have more time to get myself ready for school but I managed to get it one year ($50), so that gave me more money for my bank. We ended the services with the Bethany anthem which we found totally boring.

A 50' 38' tent was set up, with wonderful food, toys, and gifts for sale. My paternal grandmother would take me inside and buy me what I wanted. I asked her to bring Pearl to see me, because she told me she visited my sister in Allentown. I was extremely anxious and curious to meet her, but at eight years of age I was also fearful that I might not like. What if I didn't like her? My grandmother did bring her and my worries came true. She was thin, with her hair cut so short, she almost looked bald. She scared me because she looked so sad and forlorn. Her clothes looked ancient and worn, and she didn't talk. We sat under the tent sneaking looks at each other. I wanted to cry. We had nothing in common. Miss Anna didn't ask about the visit and all I told her was that it had taken place. I hadn't seen Pearl since I had been admitted to Bethany, and after that day I never saw her again until she was released from Allentown State Hospital at age eighteen when I was fifteen and she visited me on her own at Bethany. I looked for my other siblings during chapel to see if they had met her, but as usual we had no contact. They didn't visit with Pearl or me that day. It seems strange to me that Bethany never got us together. After visiting with me, my grandmother usually went to the boys' cottages to see them. Why she didn't that day I don't know. I suspect they all had to go to Bethany's farm and milk cows, which had to be done daily because we had a lot of cattle, or maybe she had to get Pearl back to Allentown.

My paternal grandmother was about 5'2" and obese. She looked almost as heavy as she was tall but I didn't care. She was the only family to ever visit. It was an embarrassment to not have family. A few of the girls had family visit every week. The time she brought Pearl to Bethany, she took a bus from her home in Reading to Allentown, then another bus from Allentown to Womelsdorf (approximately 80 miles one way). She and Pearl, age 10, walked a mile from the bus stop to the orphanage. I wonder what Pearl thought of her day. I couldn't appreciate what she had done until years later. How I wish I could now tell her what this visit, her other visits, and her gifts meant to me. I was so anxious to see her that I would go down to the front entrance of Bethany via the back road to meet her. I hope I thought to carry her bags.

My grandmother abruptly stopped coming when I was about ten years of age. I don't know why but I assume it became too physically difficult for her. No one explained her absence to me. I assume she could no longer endure the trip, but at that time, I wondered what I had done to stop her from wanting to come. I missed her. I was not informed of her death and learned of it when I visited my brother in Reading after I left Bethany. Although she only came about twice a year, the visits were so meaningful for me. It meant she cared and I was not alone in the world. Did I forget to thank her? Did I say the wrong thing?

I couldn't eat in the cottages on Anniversary Day, as the church-run dinners were expensive. My aunt (my mother's sister) and her adult child visited, but spent little time with me, as they were working in one of the kitchens serving meals. My aunt gave me $5, which I later banked because Bethany gave us $5 and my grandmother treated me. We roamed the grounds freely all day and that freedom exhilarated me.

The Ringgold Band played Sousa marches and patriotic songs during the day, except when the pageant was being performed. We had to bob and weave to walk because thousands of people were roaming the grounds, visiting and spending their money to support Bethany. The pageant area got so flooded with people that they stood all over Reed Cottage's terraced lawn, and those who couldn't find seats in the grove flowed into the orchards behind the seats.

The excitement of the day can't be described. It was over the top and better than Christmas. At bedtime I wallowed in the day's pleasantries and my depression temporarily abated.

One Anniversary Day when I was eight, I walked by what we called "the bubblers," about ten fountains of very cold water fed by a reservoir in the mountains. On the hottest of days, this water was delectable. I saw my brother, LeRoy sitting with our mother at the bubblers. In a flash I felt all kinds of emotions, mostly shock and very angry feelings that I had never felt about her before. I learned that the lovely woman I had imagined in my daydreams was overweight with swollen legs and ankles, sad looking, with no show of emotion in her face, and dressed in an ugly housedress. Worse than her looks was the fact that I felt I looked like her. That was very difficult for me to accept because it didn't jive with my mantra to not be like her. I wanted to change my looks which perhaps is why I never saw myself as pretty even though as I got into high school, I was told often how pretty I was. I never could agree. I hadn't seen her since I was placed at Bethany and I had no idea she was coming. When I think back, her five year period of not being allowed to visit had expired and maybe that is why she felt free to visit. No one told me to expect her. I felt repulsed by her. The positive feelings I had for her changed in a flash. It was as if all of them were dropped from me into the ground and

I was stripped of them, tramped on them, and killed them. The negative bond that I replaced them with, was in full bloom and existed from that day until a few years ago. Unfortunately, the messages I received from the orphanage staff about her had persuaded me that she was an awful person. It was a bond of hate, anger, shame, and hurt that replaced my good feelings. Why didn't my mother tell me she was visiting? Why didn't Miss Anna tell me? I was ashamed and crushed to see how old and heavy she looked in her housedress, and I debated whether I should join them. I wanted to rant and rave at her for abandoning us. Why didn't she care like Miss Anna did?

After the shock dissipated somewhat, I walked down to visit with her. We barely talked to one another. There were no hugs or kisses. The longer I stayed, the more disgusting she became to me. My brother offered her a coconut strip and she ate the whole piece. Her selfishness angered me, although in fairness she probably wasn't well fed and she probably never could afford candy. This moment was a turning point for me. My fantasy of a beautiful mother who missed me and cared about me was finally eradicated. No longer would I miss her or yearn for her. I loathed her and knew I had to forget her. It was an earth shattering experience and I never got over the embarrassment of having her for a mother until years later.

I got up and left her alone with my brother and didn't say goodbye. I buried all the negativity of the meeting and was happy again, or as happy as I could be after such a traumatic event. That night I told Miss Anna about the encounter but not about my feelings. I asked her why she hadn't told me my mother was coming. She said she didn't know my mother was planning to visit, but that Anniversary Day was the only day of the year anyone could visit the campus without permission. That was probably why she came on that particular day and at no other time.

We put on plays twice a year that outsiders were allowed to attend. I was the lead as long as I was at Leinbach with Miss Anna, but no family ever came to see me perform. No one clapped or praised me, as is usually done at performances. It was understood that we performed to promote Bethany. In one of the Christmas plays my underpants fell down. I kept my cool and repeated the line before mine which was," for Christmas, I want a train, a bus, and etcetera." This was of course the boy's line. But I was humiliated. Miss Anna came to my rescue and fixed my pants and I continued on because it was important for me to do it right for Bethany. I loved taking the lead and did this from six years of age until I was eight.

I was frequently both an inpatient and outpatient at the infirmary while living in Leinbach. Between ages six and eight, I developed many painful boils on my arms and back. Miss Anna told me it was because I was a poor eater. The nurse would dress them and see me every day until they opened. I lay on a sofa in the playroom to soak them and was told not to move. Being such a compliant child, I did just that.

One day as I was soaking an arm boil, a sixteen-year-old boy sat on the sofa near my head. I heard him making noises, but had no idea what he was doing. He placed his penis near my arm, scaring me half to death. I was too frightened to scream and worried that I'd get in trouble if I did. I was frozen in fear and whimpered. I had no voice to cry out. He asked me if I had never seen a boy "play with himself before?" I didn't understand the question and made no response. Fortunately for me, he went back to his chair. I was repulsed at this first sight of an adult penis. I relayed the incident to one of the girls, who repeated it to the boy's sister. She called me a liar and said if I ever lied about him again, she would personally beat me up. I never told anyone else and certainly no adults. She scared me.

Contagious diseases or high fevers sent us to the infirmary to avoid a community epidemic. When I got the mumps, I was put into isolation with two girls who also had them. The room was kept dark and only the nurse and doctor entered. It was most depressing. I looked forward to the doctor coming daily because he was so cheerful. He always had a smile and visited with me for a few minutes. Miss Barthelme, the nurse did not exude personality, but she respected our need for privacy and independence. I liked her, yet I can't describe her because I no longer can visualize her. She would sit and work jigsaw puzzles with me or anyone else in the playroom, regardless of our ages. Even now I have a jigsaw puzzle going every day in order to keep myself awake after nine p.m., because I can't sleep at night if I go to bed before eleven p.m. Our medical needs were addressed faithfully and professionally. The nurse was quiet and never intrusive. She allowed me to bathe myself and luxuriate in a tub with hot soapy water. I was accustomed to being rushed and bathing with others. I could rest in there with a book. Ah, how nice was that!

I would look out the window and see kids going to school or chapel, and I was delighted to know I didn't have those cares. I would daydream about how much better life would be after Bethany or about my anger at my mother. I felt she could care less that I was sick. At bedtime the nurse would turn out the light and even say goodnight, which the matrons didn't do except for Miss Anna.

I had a bad case of eczema on my arms, legs, and behind my ears while at Leinbach, so I was a regular outpatient from about age six through fourteen. I was treated with tar treatments or ultraviolet rays. It was all I could do to endure the itching or the treatments. If I got a tar treatment, I had to have my arms wrapped like a mummy to keep the salve on my arms and not on the bed sheets. How I detested these treatments! The nurse unwrapped me each morning, but washing the ointment would bring back the rash. What a bummer! The treatment left my arms feeling raw. I was miserable and embarrassed to have this condition; I wore only long sleeve attire for years and itched 24/7. I was told not to scratch it, but it felt better when I did-at least temporarily.

One morning as I was walking back to Leinbach, I heard a knock on the window of the boy's cottage. When I looked up, a boy was exposing himself from the waist down. I was so frightened that I ran all the way back to Miss Anna, but told no one about it because anything related to sex I felt would get me into trouble. I learned to see myself and everyone else as asexual. In my thinking no one had sexual parts. I never explored my body nor had sexual thoughts most of my years at Bethany. Now, that sounds weird to me.

If we were contagious or had high fevers, we had to live at the infirmary until we recuperated. One day while I was an inpatient at the infirmary, I saw a girl from Leinbach being carried out of her bed and taken downstairs. No one told me why. The next day I found out she was dead. The bully told me I had killed her when I cut a cowlick in her bangs. I believed her and feared what my punishment would be. I rued what I had done, but knew I had not done it on purpose. We were taken to the funeral but I couldn't look at her out of guilt. I confessed to Mr. Stoltzfus, the school principal, what I had done because I could not carry the guilt anymore, it was killing me, and he told me she died of a kidney disease. Phew! The relief was beyond belief.

My last year at Leinbach was more peaceful. My bully had moved to Santee, as she was older than I. I didn't want to leave Miss Anna, but I knew I was going to leave for Santee soon because I was about to enter third grade and it was forbidden to live in the same cottage as your third grade teacher. I dreaded that I would have to live with my bully without Miss Anna's support.

I felt so sad, lost, and alone the day I had to leave. What I didn't know was that my bully was now in a clique of six who viewed me as their target.

I never formally said goodbye to Miss Anna. When an older girl took my belongings and me from Leinbach's playroom, Miss Anna was upstairs. It was extremely hard to leave her. If I had cried in her presence, she would have told me in a matter of fact way to stop crying because the move was inevitable. I had to go. I wonder if she felt the same pain and hurt I felt. I would like to think that's why she didn't say goodbye. I felt a deep bond between us, but didn't understand bonding at that time. The loss was almost more than I could handle. Writing now about this separation is so difficult that I've had to stop and take a break. I knew that was the end of our relationship and it was. I saw her one more time when my husband and I visited her in Phoebe Home, a nursing home. She denied any special feelings for me and said she just paid more attention to those that needed it the most.

I was devastated about leaving, but the older girls had no tolerance for tears. I felt like a cow walking to slaughter. My feet didn't want to move. I buried my feelings of hurt, fear, and anger, where they remained for years. Even though we were not in touch, I never forgot her.

At this time in my life I was unable to appreciate joy or love even though I felt them. I would not have supposed that Miss Anna would miss me. I felt like a nonentity floating on a cloud, watching real people but I was a hollow shell. I kept all these feelings to myself and felt like such a non-person and so unseen. Why would Miss Anna miss me? At Bethany all highs were considered bragging and lows were ignored. I was depressed and acting almost like a robot. I had no identity and simply put one foot in front of the other to survive. I went where I had to go and did what I had to do, without any understanding of what I was feeling. Bragging was almost a crime. This was another part of my Pennsylvania Dutch upbringing.

Chapter Five

MR. STOLTZFUS, A PHI BETA KAPPA Mennonite, was the principal of our K through 8 school which was housed in a lovely stone building. We attended classes from eight to four every day, with two short recesses and an hour for lunch. Boys came and went out the back door, while girls used the front door. Every evening, fifth through eighth grades, we had a study hour at school supervised by the third grade teacher where talking to each other was prohibited. The walls were opened between the two upstairs rooms and she sat where she could watch all four grades at one time. Mr. Stoltzfus lived on campus, but as the principal didn't take a turn at supervision of the study hour unless the teacher was sick. We felt compelled to do what we were assigned to do and more so if he was there. We would sneak whispers behind the teacher's back but not when Mr. Stoltzfus was there. We were not as motivated to do the things required of us when she supervised because she wasn't as observant as he was.

Each floor of the school had two large rooms with two grades per room. The dentist was on the first floor, and from fifth through eighth grade, I was responsible for bringing him patients and assisting at his chair every Friday. I had to take responsibility for any assigned homework I missed that day. The idea of evaluating whether I liked the job or not never entered my mind. It was a career path Bethany chose for me. Today, children in care, don't get any career training as we got at Bethany. Bethany sent some of the boys at 15 to Stevens Trading School to try to give them a career to pursue.

The upstairs had a wooden sliding wall between the two rooms. It was opened each morning for songs and the pledge of allegiance. Most of the songs were patriotic. If it was opened at any other time, it meant trouble for someone, because they wanted all of us to see infractions being punished. After the wall was closed, our classes began. One grade in each room worked at an assignment at their desks while the other grade in the room was being taught.

Boys and girls had classes together, but my siblings were never in the same classes with me. I saw them if our paths crossed, but we never interacted. Since boys and girls entered from different sides of the building, it was hard to have contact, and by now we were not into relating to each other. It had been too long since we had been a family and I was already eleven years old.

Occasionally we would see each other at recess time, but basically we had stopped even thinking of each other. I once got to talk to my older brother, LeRoy and was so excited by this contact. I wanted to show him a letter I received from our oldest brother, who was in the Pacific theater during World War II. He took it from me and tore it up. I have no idea why he did this. I was so crushed that I ran to Mr. Stoltzfus and reported him. I can't remember if he got punished, but I know I cried over that loss. The letter had made me feel that I had a family somewhere out there.

There was a small library where Mr. Stoltzfus had his office. It was barely a library or an office as it was a tiny room. The library books were very limited and we used mostly encyclopedias as references stored in our classrooms. We barely saw him during first through fourth grades because he didn't teach those grades. His classes were fifth through eighth. We were vaguely aware that he was the "boss." I was impressed that this stern, unsmiling "boss" smiled at me so often. Not a big smile, but the corners of his mouth curled up somewhat. Little did I know how strongly he would impact on my entire life!

Mr. Stoltzfus could be stern and tough with the kids he didn't like. My brother, LeRoy was one he didn't like. He dressed up like Hitler one Halloween at the suggestion of his matron, and Mr. Stoltzfus wasn't amused. He called him many names, including "unpatriotic." I now believe he nurtured those he thought would be successful and picked on those he didn't expect to make a success in their lives. Years later, after my brother left Bethany, Mr. Stoltzfus apologized to him for assuming he would be a loser as my brother became an important politician in Reading.

Grade 1 through 8 with Mr. Stoltzfus as principal.

My first grade teacher left no impression on me. I don't remember her appearance, her classes, or any moment of my time there. Years later I visited Mr. Rohrbach and his wife asked me who my kindergarten teacher was. I told her that I only remembered I didn't like her. She then proclaimed that she was that teacher. I felt awful about what I said and wanted to fall into a pit, so when she asked about the teacher who taught me first and second grade I told her I couldn't remember her either. That cut the tension in the room but I felt guilty for what I had said. That feeling of guilt still creeps into my life many times and even when the other guy is at fault. I still don't know who taught my two first years.

My third and fourth grade teacher had a presence that said "I'm all business" in a condescending manner. I feared her before I got to her grades as she was the teacher I had known in

Miss Anna's cottage. She was a tad overweight, well-dressed, attractive woman but very intimidating. She didn't seem to like me, but neither did she treat me any differently than she did the other kids. School was serious and no fun. Even celebrations were done "properly." There was no nonsense in her room which made school very boring.

I got so sick of the same old songs we sang every morning, but swallowed my rebellious feelings because it would have been disastrous to express them. I was tired of routine and even today I can't stand the same old activities every day.

Art classes were my nemesis and I still won't attempt to draw. The few times I have tried, all the old feelings return and I freeze so I don't attempt it any more. Our mean art teacher came to Bethany once a week and taught all grades. When I was in third grade, he drew a picture on the blackboard every week and we had to copy it exactly as he had done it. One week it was a rabbit. I struggled with it but just couldn't get it. He accused me of not trying and I was devastated that he didn't appreciate how hard I had tried. I never attempted to draw anything again and I cheated, cried, or faked my way through art classes, right through high school.

Every week we memorized a poem and got graded for how well we recited them. That was easier for me than art. I can still repeat parts of some of those poems, including the one we all heard during the war: "In Flanders Fields." I remember this one because I felt what its meaning was so strongly.

Fifth grade through eighth was a whole different story. Mr. Stoltzfus taught history and geography, so I had him as a teacher twice a day. Mr. Rohrbach taught Math and English. Bethany stressed excellence in hiring teachers, so they were top notch. Mr. Rohrbach was stern but not mean and very serious. He didn't relate to any of us except when he taught. He and Mr. Stoltzfus worked well together, and we knew not to criticize one to the other. Neither one would hear it.

One day when I was in sixth grade, I was not paying attention to Mr. Stoltzfus and he called me to the front of the class and spanked me over his knee with a piece of a broad wooden paddle. He didn't spank hard but you sure were intimidated in front of the class. I cried because I could not hold back the tears through the humiliation. My crying was humiliating too. He then felt sorry and he had me sit on his lap for the rest of that period in front of the whole class. It soothed me on the outside but I was very angry at him inside. My anger dissipated by morning and life went on.

Mr. Stoltzfus liked me very much. Recesses were a total joy. He would play Chinese checkers with me almost every day. No one else had this privilege. He would hug me at times and was always so fatherly with me. He told me he had singled me out because when I was a preschooler in Reed Cottage, he could see from the upstairs windows of the school. He had watched me play in the snow on the front terraces in a bright red snowsuit with my deep black hair coming out of my cap. He noticed I usually played alone and seemed to be self-directed.

In our supervised evening study hour until seventh grade, I did whatever homework was required. That year I decided to read all I could about the Renaissance, the Reformation, and early Greek history, which is when I fell in love with the Oracles of Delphi. This took precedence over homework. Mr. Stoltzfus warned me to stop daydreaming and get to my assignments because I was always looking out the window. He told me there were no knights in shining armor coming to rescue me. Little did he realize that I was thinking about my horrible shameful mother and wishing I were old enough to be out of Bethany and be my own person. Somehow I had the sense to believe him and quit daydreaming, but I never gave up the thought that somewhere out there things would be better but I did give up my academics. I knew I had to save myself because there was no one to fall back on if I failed myself.

I continued to study my own interests in school despite the warning that I might flunk. I assumed it wouldn't happen, but like a bolt from the sky, I found I had done just that. It was a blow I couldn't live with or tell anyone about. I felt so ashamed. Looking back, I feel that unconsciously I wanted to flunk. Why would I want to be promoted to eighth grade and leave Mr. Stoltzfus? He wasn't angry with me for flunking, or at least not to my face. I went back to seventh grade in the fall and although I felt humiliated around my former classmates, who were now in the same room but in eighth grade, we continued our relationship as if nothing had changed.

I was so full of problems and very depressed. Flunking added to my discontent. My feelings were so intense; I was so alert to my surroundings and observed everything around me to avoid surprises and conflicts. I had enough without adding to my misery. The whole world felt unsafe. Yet I couldn't make myself talk to anyone, including Mr. Stoltzfus. I was walking around in a fog and the sadness overwhelmed me. Death would have been welcome—not by suicide, but from a disease. I could barely survive the bullies. To me, they were just like today's terrorists. They never physically hurt me, but they would laugh at me, hurl slurs, and criticize me every chance they had. It was constant and overwhelming.

All my insides were churned up to the point that I thought I was going crazy. I hurt from the top of my head all the way down to my toes. My desperation was so intense that I can hardly think of it now. Little did I realize that I could have talked to Mr. Stoltzfus. He would have taken care of the bullies permanently. I was too afraid it would be worse for me in the cottage if I ratted on them. Now I realize that the bullies would have been fearful of harassing me because Mr. Stoltzfus commanded such respect and authority. He seemed to read both my emotional and educational needs, and could do the same for the rest of the kids, but he was unaware of my bullying problem because the bullies behaved during school. They waited until we were in the unsupervised playrooms in Santee's basement. I wanted so much to be with him 24/7 because he was my only protecting support. I craved parents who would listen to me and understand what I said. He never knew I would sit on the steps alone across from his room at night, cry, and yearn to be with him or for him to look out of his window (which I never saw him do) and smile at me. The psychological pain was excruciating and almost unbearable. Nothing since has been as painful as those days were.

Art classes were still a problem for me. One day, when I was ten and in fifth grade, I was caught reading a book behind my drawing board. The girl behind me was drawing a picture for me while I was reading. I was sent to Mr. Stoltzfus's office, where he was meeting with the superintendent of the Berks County Schools. Through my tears of humiliation and shame, I had to explain why I was there. He gently turned me around and told me to go back to class and do as I was told. We never talked about the incident again. He knew being sent to the awesome superintendent there was punishment enough. We all assumed the superintendent was the most important man on earth and we gave him credit for more responsibility for us than he actually had.

In sixth grade I witnessed another side of Mr. Stoltzfus. My oldest brother was in eighth grade. The sliding wall opened in early afternoon, so I knew there was a problem. A large tub of soapy water with a washcloth and towel were placed in view for all four grades to see. Mr. Stoltzfus asked my brother to step forward and strip to the waist which he did. Mr. Stoltzfus proceeded to bathe him, remarking that this is what happened to children who came to school dirty. I was angry at him and humiliated for my sibling. My humiliation surprised me because I felt I didn't even know my brother. Why should I feel badly? But I told myself, *"He's your brother, so somehow it reflects on you!"* I felt anger at Mr. Stoltzfus, but we never discussed it. We never discussed any feelings. Remember, we were both Pennsylvania Dutch.

I want to clarify that not one child, to my knowledge, ever experienced any sexual inappropriateness with staff or each other at Bethany. Mr. Stoltzfus was always an appropriate father figure and we had little physical contact. In Chinese checkers I had to win honestly. He was almost a saint to me, but I detested the demeaning and hurtful side of him. He made my survival possible, and through him I was able to know I would one day have a better life because he showed me a different life than what I was experiencing.

When we played Chinese checkers, he would tell me about the war. He was worried early on that we would lose. The Japanese were seizing many of the Pacific islands. I didn't worry, because if the Japanese conquered us, I knew Mr. Stoltzfus would protect me. My magical thinking was florid and pervasive about many things. One day he told us Uncle Sam had called him to serve our country. I walked through the woods crying and singing "My Buddy":

Nights are long since you went away.
I think about you all through the day
My buddy, my buddy, etc.

Being compelled to serve was every young man's duty and Mr. Stoltzfus was no exception. That was what the draft meant. It seemed an eternity before he told us Uncle Sam considered his job more important than serving in the military. I cared so deeply for him, even fantasized about marrying him so I could be with him forever. I wish I had told him before he died of Alzheimer's disease how greatly he influenced me, but I only saw him once after I left Bethany— at Mr. Rohrbach's funeral. He smiled at me, but we didn't speak because I was waiting for him to approach me. Many people approached him. I was still depressed and felt unworthy of such a great man. It is one of my deepest regrets that we didn't speak and I never got to tell him how important a part he played in my life. At this stage of my life I was feeling like a nonentity and so insignificant. I wasn't worthy of his time. I wonder what he thought when he saw me.

I moved on to eighth grade the following fall. Except for the anticipated separation, it was an easier year for me. My tormenter was now in high school, so I never saw her anymore. She had also moved to a different cottage. I had my first crush on Bethany's farmer's son. He was cute, but not too swift mentally, and I cringed each time Mr. Stoltzfus demeaned him. I was studying hard and tried to help him get good grades, but he was hopeless.

One Friday afternoon I was told to leave school and go back to Santee to pack a bag for the weekend. Mr. Stoltzfus informed me that my mother was at the office, waiting to take me to her home for the weekend. I begged him not to make me go. His suggestion was that I should go and tell him all about it on Monday. He convinced me and reluctantly I went.

Seeing her in the office didn't shock me, because she looked as frumpy as when I had last seen her six years previously on Anniversary Day. We didn't speak a word to each other, even when we got to the car. We left in a beat up Model T Ford driven by my mother's female friend. I kept looking out the window and thinking about how I would miss Bethany. The driver and my mother talked. I tuned them out because I felt so sad and bewildered. We arrived at my mother's rental home, which she shared with a common-law husband and their three girls, ranging in age from about seven to four. I don't know where their three girls were but they were not with my mother that weekend. I am now aware of the effort she made to connect with me but I refused her.

They were not as poor as when we lived with her, but they didn't have money to spare. My mother went food shopping on Saturday and bought me a penny lollipop, which made her common-law husband very angry. He felt it was an extravagant gesture. I was humiliated at his treatment of my mother but my mother told me to go ahead and eat it so I did. Common law husbands were men who lived with one woman for seven years which made them legally married. He was an engineer and worked for the city of Reading. I was afraid of him and sensed I shouldn't trust him. Until then, all the men I knew were clean-shaven. This man had a moustache. That added to my fear, but I can't explain why. His talk to me was filthy and inappropriate with sex on his mind all the time. My mother never left us in a room by ourselves, but neither could she shut him up. I felt half sick to my stomach all weekend. Maybe she cared?

My mother put me to bed and went downstairs. Soon her slimy husband approached my bed and started to talk to me. I was so terrified that I don't know what he said. I remained quiet as per usual, but I felt like running away from him or kicking him. When I think back to that time, I realize I never thought to call out. I was accustomed to not being heard. I pulled the sheet tight over my body. My mother sensed a problem and came to my rescue. She chased him downstairs and he never returned to my bedroom. I didn't realize at the time that this was an act of caring on my mother's part. Did she love me? Perhaps. It certainly was a welcome surprise. I felt she had to have some feeling for me, even though she talked little. Yet I was angry at her lack of attention during all those years at Bethany. I wanted nothing from her and neither did I want to give her anything. I mostly felt disgust and shame toward her and her husband. They were the pits, but I consoled myself that a weekend couldn't last forever. I still remind myself that everything is time limited. I can't remember her asking about my life, and neither one of us spoke to each other very much the whole weekend. She and her common-law husband interacted, but I can't tell you a word they said. I just wanted out of there.

What a relief to get back to Bethany. Mr. Stoltzfus asked on Monday about the weekend. I told him I hated it but didn't elaborate. I was too embarrassed to recount what my mother's husband had done or of the filthy words he spoke to me. They were so bad that I can't repeat them here but I never forgot them. I told him I never wanted to go back and he sent me directly to the superintendent's office to reiterate my feelings. We never visited again. Did my mother know of my wishes or did she simply never request that I visit? I don't know.

Let me digress for a moment and tell you that years later my mother wanted to divorce this man. She told me she believed she was hexed by him, another Pennsylvania Dutch phenomenon. She paid five dollars a visit to someone who claimed she could break the hex. When she was no longer hexed she was able to divorce.

In the spring, for two years, I would go to the woods to pick blueberries for Mr. Stoltzfus and he would pay me fifty cents a quart. Giant anthills almost as tall as me surrounded the berries. Eventually they would bite me and that was the end of picking berries for the day. I would run down to the cottage screaming and then change my clothes because there were so many ants on them. I banked the money and never told him about the ants. I felt so honored to do this for him and loved making money. I thought money was going to be part of my salvation when I left Bethany.

Chapter Six

THE MOST DEVASTATING PLACEMENT I experienced during my entire time at Bethany was living at Santee Hall at age eight. I seemed to be the only person who was being bullied, but I never asked myself why, but it was a daily ugly phenomenon. Maybe it was because I was given many significant responsibilities because staff felt I was reliable. I was so afraid of bullies and resented that I was so afraid. No one had a relationship with Mr. Stoltzfus or Miss Anna like mine. I was also the smallest and slightest built in the cottage. I remain only five feet tall. Maybe these were the reasons I was so picked on. This made for difficult times when we were in the basement playrooms. Every day was a day of desperation, fear, and utter despair. No place on the earth would have been as bleak and I was overwhelmed. My mistake was not talking to Mr. Stoltzfus about the bullying and my despair. He would never have accepted that behavior from anyone. I understand now that I made my own misery.

A bright spot for me was Margie who was also at Santee and we became close. My respite from the bullies was to go to the dormitory and hide under the bed to read the romance magazines she supplied from her father's house. We did this together and kept very quiet if staff walked through the dorm. We seldom got caught but neither did we have time to read without sneaking the time. There was too much work to be done. If we were ever seen idle, we were assigned a task. There was always something they could find to keep us busy so we tried to stay hidden.

The main kitchen was on the first floor, with the dining room across the hall from it. Boys and girls had separate living quarters but ate together in that dining room. A matron patrolled the aisle to keep girls and boys apart. My younger brothers were there while I was, but I had given up on looking for them. It didn't even cross my mind.

Santee had a spacious laundry for the whole institution and we ironed and worked the huge dangerous ironing mangle. At least it was dangerous for kids, but we ironed sheets and tablecloths on it with supervision. We also had a drawing room for visitors which rarely was used and a small living room for us to await assignments or to relax for ten minutes before dinner. Our dorms were on the third and fourth floors. Located on the third floor was a sewing room where we darned socks (how I hated darning), the cook's bedroom, and a large space to store our clothes and change outfits. A small room under the steps leading to the basement was the designated "egg room," where we sorted and packaged our farm's eggs for delivery to the main kitchen. The most important place for us was the basement, where our lockers and two playrooms were located, as well as food storage. The playrooms were important because we spent a good part of our day there and that was where I dreaded going. Because we were unsupervised, the bullies could have a heyday with me and tormented me beyond description. You can't imagine my despair, it ran so deep. I couldn't allow myself to feel such horror. I hid my feelings or I think I would have gone crazy. They were safely hidden within me as a means of self-protection.

Santee on the left – Boys on the right. Note the large breezeway between the buildings.

Connected to Santee was a spacious breezeway that contained the chapel, which all kids five and older attended every night. Bethany was a United Church of Christ establishment, so all of us belonged to that church and were admitted to Bethany on that premise.

Each time we went down into the basement we made a lot of noise on the steps to scare any rats running freely about. Opening our lockers was another test of courage—we immediately jumped back in case a rat jumped out. Once it happened to me and it was terrifying. They were attracted by the bread room, the canning room, and a room for donated food. These were huge rats, not mice!

Our code of ethics was tight and almost sacred. We never told on each other unless it was a dire necessity because there would have been hell to pay from our peers. I suppose that was why I never told Mr. Stoltzfus about my terrorists. Twice I broke the code but only because I was reacting to dire circumstances. One time I told a matron about a desperate sobbing girl who was attempting to slit her wrists with scissors while in the basement. She was taken to the infirmary, but was returned to Santee and she never attempted it again. The other time I will tell you about later.

I was ten when a boy of the same age snuck into the Santee basement, gently pushed me against a wall, kissed me on the mouth, and then fled. I was stunned, aghast, and so naïve I never connected it with romance or sexuality. When we saw each other on campus after that, we never spoke about it. He was a nice shy kid and so I never expected a kiss from him or anyone else. Of course, I didn't tell any adult because coming into girl's space was a no- no. Amazing about how little we shared with each other or with staff or maybe it was only me.

We had two playrooms. The clique of six bullies used the large playroom, so I used the small one. It was not my choice, but that was my only respite for as long as it lasted. If they felt like harassing me, they came as a group to the smaller playroom. Their numbers alone terrified me not to mention their own anger at their own situations; add the chiding and accusations, and I felt myself melt into a small blob. I wanted to fade away, but I quietly took it. Death would have been welcome. The depth of my pain, terror, and despair is indescribable. It is an amazing phenomenon that you learn not to feel to protect yourself, but you survive without living. I already felt like a nonperson and the emptiness stayed with me for years.

Recreational activities were planned all summer, with the superintendent's daughter as the director. We played games outside or made arts and crafts for Bethany to sell on Anniversary Day. She appointed me leader of my age group, with assignments for us every day. My tormenters took advantage of the situation and I was a sitting duck. They terrified me with threats of physical abuse and harassment. I was beaten down and fearful even before I assumed this role and the misery got worse each day for me. I wanted to disappear into quicksand so my despair would go away. I pleaded with the recreational leader to remove this responsibility from my shoulders. I told her I couldn't take the abuse anymore. Her response was a tap on my head and a brisk command: "I know you can do it, so go back and do your job." I was paralyzed with feelings of anger and powerlessness. I had finally spoken up and wasn't heard. There was no one to turn to and I was absolutely a basket case. There were six of them against me and I don't believe they were ever told to stop the harassing. Did any adult even know about it? I doubt it. I was beyond devastated and felt absolutely hopeless.

In this same year my worst bully was meeting me after school each day to check my underpants for any dampness. They were usually damp because I was too shy to put my hand up in front of the boys and request going to the bathroom. I had to sit openly in the gazebo near the school and pull my pants down so she could feel them. She would report to the whole playroom that they were damp and then I would be shamed each time. She had taken care of our laundry and found my damp pants on one occasion and that was the impetus to check each day. I would stall leaving school but never seemed to be late enough to avoid her. I can't tell you how devastating this whole experience was for me. I had to walk from the gazebo to the playroom knowing full well that I was going to be attacked. My defense was to look toward town and tell myself, "Somewhere out there, life will be better." I still believed it, which kept me going. But it didn't help me in the present moment and I was almost beyond coping.

Gazeebo where my pants were checked and reservoir which supplied water for the bubblers.

Two years later, four of my worst tormenters moved on to the next cottage. I was eleven years old. My last year at Santee offered me relief except for the two left behind. They were the weakest of the six unless the uninvolved kids in the playroom sided with the bullies and that did happen at times. If no one else was around, I could walk away from them or threaten to report them. I would never have threatened them when all six were there.

One Saturday night during the war our movie was cancelled. We knelt by our beds and said our prayers before climbing into bed. Suddenly all the lights went on, and we were told to get dressed and go to the basement. I was about twelve years of age. I knew the Japanese were coming up our front road to conquer Bethany and I was terrified. But I steeled myself to act bravely and believed I could scare them away. After we were all in the basement, we were told to put on our coats and walk to the auditorium to see the movie. What a relief I felt! Why hadn't someone told us what was going on? The movie had been delivered after all. Phew!

As at Leinbach, holidays were celebrated at Santee. By now, another wonderful experience occurred—we were all given $5 to shop in Reading for Christmas presents. I knew the stores through Miss Anna, so I knew where to go to do window shopping or which store had the most beautiful decorations. The Five-and-Ten was my ultimate goal, so I could buy the most gifts for my money, including a handkerchief for Mr. Stoltzfus. On the bus home we would show off what we had stolen. It was understood we would all steal or take the heat for not doing it. Some kids stole shoes or dresses and they were heroes. I was too scared to steal anything but small items from the Five-and-Ten. There were no surveillance cameras in those days, so shoplifting was less complicated. The bus was unsupervised except for the driver. He rarely ratted on us.

We attended Sunday school in the morning and church after lunch, with chapel every night. I joined the choir and sang at every church service. Most Sunday afternoons the choir boarded the bus to sing in United Church of Christ churches mostly located in the coal regions in Schuylkill County. They were located about two hours from Bethany and we went to a different one each week. We sang in the late afternoon and had dinner individually in someone's home from the congregation. They were strangers to us so it was a bit awkward. The families were lower middle class families and I suspect it was hard for some families to feed extra people. The offering taken up after our singing went to Bethany. We got home, depending on the location of the church, between ten and twelve at night that is if the bus didn't break down which it occasionally did. But we still had to get our weary bodies up early the next day and get to school on time. On one trip, I wore a full length mink coat to visit the church and family. It had been donated to Bethany and fortunately I could wear it. The moment I got back on the bus I was told nicely by the superintendent never to do that again because it made the congregation question Bethany's needs. The bus was fun for me because I could eavesdrop on conversations or sleep. The superintendent went along but I didn't join in conversations because I had learned to keep everything inside of me and shared nothing with anyone. Whatever you said could eventually be used against you. That was true during my entire stay at Bethany. Self- protection was again of a major concern for me. Being raised without parents and having to provide your own protection and safety meant not bonding with anyone. I became numb and devoid of any feelings of love or recognition of love. We were not told what a good job we had done. I suppose this is why I find it difficult to accept praise even now.

    The superintendent became our superintendent when I was about 11 years old. The one who left Bethany was a scary ugly looking man who was very tough on us. He left when he decided to marry the cook. They deserved each other as they were both mean. If he caught us in the orchards stealing fruit or stealing cherries from the back road trees, we were punished by having to stand without touching walls, in the third floor hall of Santee and memorizing a chapter from the bible. I remember being there so long that I feel asleep. I was awakened and told to complete my memorizing. Sometimes we were there for hours.

The new superintendent, Rev. Vandervere, was superintendent. He was a short about 5'2' man and slightly overweight. He was a minister and had been raised at Bethany until he was adopted by a member of Bethany's board. We would complain to him and we were heard but he didn't necessarily do as we requested. His wife was a scary person (even he was afraid to cross her) and was tough on any mistakes we made. He never went against her. If we passed her on the walkways, we would bury our heads and walk by. We often wondered how they ever decided to marry.

If we wanted to go to Robesonia for the movie and switch with the boy's night, he would listen when we explained that we wanted the Shirley Temple movie and the boys could have the cowboy one the next week. Our first superintendent would never had said yes. In fact, we would have been afraid to ask him because he looked scary with piles of keys around his waist and his ugly looks.

My first job at Santee was to scrub the floor of the main kitchen, where most food was prepared for the cottages. I did this after our school study hour which was over at 8PM. Sometimes I was so tired I didn't think I could do it, but the task wasn't negotiable. How I hated these dirty jobs! I can still see the thick dirt in the area of the stoves and the dishwasher which I thought was such a cool machine. I would turn on the light and quickly duck out of the room so the rats and roaches would scamper away before I cleaned. The big roaches didn't necessarily run away. They sure were there in spades. I did my job well to avoid demerits. They were reflected in your allowance, and I was a compulsive saver who couldn't risk a job half done. At Leinbach we got two cents a week but now we were getting a dime.

Two girls and I were assigned to peel potatoes with a mechanical peeler. We were taught to keep the eyes in the potatoes so we didn't waste any edible part of the potato as they had to feed the whole campus. We would then pick out the eyes after we stopped the machine. One day we intentionally kept the potatoes in the machine too long so we had no eyes to remove. We were hauled out of school to redo the job correctly. The cook wanted us to see how wasteful we had been. I laughed to myself about the incident because I felt I had gotten back at the cook, whom no one liked because she was mean.

The pots and pans were heavy and bigger than me, but needed to be washed. I was assigned this task even though I weighed about sixty pounds at that time. I sobbed because I couldn't manage them. I couldn't even lift them into the deep sink. I didn't have the nerve to tell the cook I was unable to handle such large ones. We never rebelled about any work assignments because what it got us was extra chores. Fortunately, the cook saw my quandary, understood, and gave me another job. Her understanding shocked me.

Once a week I had to iron a bundle of men's and boys' shirts along with about nine other girls. We had ten ironing boards and twenty flat irons heated on a gas stove that cooled too fast to complete a shirt and then it took so long for them to heat up again. By then, the shirts had dried. We begged for electric irons, but to no avail. It was a terrible waste of time, as we could never get one shirt finished before the irons cooled. The other problem was that the irons were too hot once we took them off the stove. As a result we scorched shirts, which meant rewashing them by hand and ironing them again. Under these circumstances we could never do a good job and that frustrated me because I was addicted to the thinking I had to do everything perfectly. Today, if I feel unsatisfied with food I cook, I must do it over the next day to be sure it is "perfect." Instead of acknowledging our problem, staff accused us of being lousy workers.

From the ironing room we watched our cows being led to their slaughter. It was a terrible thing to see—they sensed what was going to happen and panicked. The farmers almost carried them into the slaughter room. Then we heard a shot. When the slaughterhouse door reopened, we saw a cow suspended by its back legs and being butchered. Most of the meat was converted into hamburger, as these were the Depression years and that was the best way to stretch it. Only after I served on Bethany's board did I learn of their constant concern about feeding us because of tight budgets and the depression. No wonder wasting food was a cardinal sin.

I saw sausage and scrapple being made and still can't eat them. One day I pretended to eat my sausage and threw each bite under my chair. I was brought back from school (and missed classes) to be served another helping of that nasty sausage. They let me get away with not eating it because they knew they couldn't keep me in the dining room when dinner was being served, but I knew not to do that again. Henceforth, I gave it to another girl.

A personable low key baker was located on the second floor above the butcher. Behind his back we called him "hairy arms" because occasionally we found a hair in his cookies. We picked out the hair and ate them with great gusto. His bread was awesome. At times we got to eat it fresh baked and warm, but they rationed us because our appetites were insatiable. He tried so hard to get me to understand that the older one gets, the more ages you can relate to but I couldn't get it because everyone around me was my age and I wanted proof of what he said through arithmetic. When he gave you a cookie, you knew he was saying, "time to go" and we would leave. He was a very kind man.

I had only one visitor while in Santee when I was thirteen. It was Mr. Bowman, who stopped by for a very short time. I was listening to a radio program by myself. He came up to me and asked, "Do you know where Bertha Gensemer is?" When I said, "That's me," he asked if I recognized him and I said I did. I remember wondering, "If you liked me all these years, why didn't you come and visit and why didn't you recognize me?" I said very little. I was not interested in him or his wife anymore, if ever. As you will see, I never changed my mind about them and for good reasons. They never visited again until I was close to graduating from high school.

Summertime was not much fun. A dreaded event was being called to the kitchen in the late afternoon. That meant husking corn, snapping green beans, canning fruit, peeling onions, washing potatoes, and more. Each of these chores took hours because we had to do enough for 257 kids and staff. Sometimes, only a few of us were called because the work was only preparing enough food for staff and not as much help was needed. I was always called because of my consistent reliability. I resented giving up swimming to gratify staff, but I never overtly complained.

We cleaned every building from ceiling to floor. To scrub the ceilings, we stood on planks supported between two ladders. Although I was the runt of the group, I performed all these tasks without any machinery or long-handled mops, even at eight years of age.

If we had no school due to a snow day, these same chores were assigned to us. We were unsupervised until inspection time. While we worked, we bitched, gossiped, and fought with slackers. We did our own work well because we knew the inspection was coming; if we didn't pass inspection, we would be sent back to do it over. We cleaned all the buildings except the boys' cottages. Heaven help us if we mingled with boys! My anger was often evident in my expression, but I was told to wipe the negativity off my face and I did. Keeping us busy during these years was legitimate because Bethany couldn't afford more staff nor could they afford professional cleaners. Remember there was a depression going on and staff worked for little more than room and board.

We bathed two at a time in one tub. Two older girls washed us and would comment on our bodies. Deja vu from Leinbach. The first time I saw pubic hair I was repulsed. I was told it would happen to me, but I decided I wouldn't allow that. As it happened, I was very late maturing.

Our dormitory was on the third floor. Suddenly age did not determine who moved to the fourth floor, as younger girls than I were being moved upstairs before me. I felt very overlooked and resentful. I told the matron this was not fair and the answer I got was, "Someday you'll understand." I had buried all thoughts of sexuality, so I never knew or entertained any idea of bodily changes. I saw a younger girl move up to the fourth floor and one of the girls asked me why. I said, "I don't know but they gave her a pile of cloths." No one got Kotex in those days, only bulky large cotton cloth pads which were pinned to your underpants. I had no idea what they were for, but I had my mouth washed out with soap for telling about the cloths. How did both staff and girls keep menstruation such a deep secret? Maybe my good friend Margie knew about it but I sure didn't nor would she tell me if she knew. No one talked about it.

For a year I served lunch to the teaching staff. They had a table for eight separated from the rest of the staff but in the same room. The third grade teacher expected perfection from me. She chided me in front of all the teachers if I made a mistake. When she nagged, Mr. Stoltzfus smiled at me but kept silent. At times I would go to the adjoining room and cry. I was relieved to leave this job and knew I would never again waitress. The only good thing about it was listening to their gossip about their families they had visited but no talk of criticism of the orphanage or staff.

Because I had not started menstruating, I was transferred to Reed, the baby cottage. This was done to hide the fact that I was obviously too old for the third floor at Santee, but not yet ready for the fourth floor. I dreaded the idea of moving—Reed was still under the supervision of the matron I had disliked as a small child, and the twenty-five kids ranged in age from infancy to age five were there. I was thirteen and it was 1943. I loathed this transfer, but it was a decision carved in stone. It did separate me from my bullies though.

Chapter Seven

LIKE SANTEE, REED COTTAGE was a miserable two-year placement. I dealt with it as I had dealt with much of my unhappiness—my mind became foggy, as if a shade was pulled over my brain. I couldn't face the terror I was to experience. If only I could tell a mother how I felt. I craved parents and craved them for all my years at Bethany. Only at school was my thinking somewhat clear, because I felt it was a safe place. A feeling of safety is still a big need of mine. I often dream that there's someone under my bed who's going to take me away. Fred wakes me up from my nightmare, and then I'm aware that I'm safe. Each year this dream seems to occur less frequently. I am not afraid of the dark but I don't like it if I can have light so I can see all around me to protect myself. After all I had only me to depend on. That is no longer true.

The kids' daily routine remained as it had been when I lived at Reed as a young child, and the matron didn't like me any better. My mother was my crime and the matron would say, "You'll be just like her." No wonder I was hell bent not to be like her or the matron! But I had some freedom when I went upstairs where we slept away from all staff and kids.

My fogging over let me survive but also blocked all feelings. Thank goodness I had Mr. Stoltzfus as a teacher, even though I didn't share my unhappiness with him. I smiled through my pain my whole childhood but continued to block feelings. I never gave up on finding the happiness I craved. I would look out the window and tell myself that somewhere out there it would be better. I kept watching the calendar for when I could leave Reed, and it felt like never. I daydreamed about a better life for myself when I was supposed to be watching the angry kids. I detested that part of my job more than any I had before or after this one. I wanted to strike out at every infraction because my anger was eating me up. When I wiped their faces after breakfast, I pushed hard if they gave me a hard time or if I was having a bad day, just as had been done to me.

After wiping their faces, I carried two buckets of about thirty dirty diapers to the basement. I had to rinse them by hand (what an odiferous, dirty job), wash them in a wringer type machine, rinse them twice, run them through the wringer twice, hang them outside regardless of the weather, and take them inside when I came home from school. Sometimes I only rinsed them once because I wanted to get back at the matron or I was in a hurry to get ready for school. While I was in the many roomed basement, I imagined a man watching me. Sometimes I checked the other empty rooms and rushed through the job to get out of there. It was all in my imagination, but I wasn't aware of that at the time. I think that we had heard many times that "bums" slept in our playrooms in Santee's basement overnight. I doubt that was true but I believed it at the time. All the rooms were dark except for the laundry room which had an overhead light. I felt unsafe as if someone would carry me off and I felt the man watching me was a dangerous villain.

Ironing the kids' and matron's clothes was my after school activity. There were no synthetic fabrics at that time so ironing was an ongoing project. The nagging matron continually walked past the door to make sure I wasn't slacking off. I wanted to scorch her ugly house dresses, but I knew better. My anger was so close to the surface that I had to hold my tongue rather than tell her off. Had I acted out my anger, she would have piled on more work and might have sent me to the superintendent who would have doled out some punishment.

I ate dinner with the other older girl assigned there. After getting the kids to the dining room we were not allowed to talk while we ate at a separate table from the kids, so we could finish before the kids. Meanwhile, the cook and matron chatted away all through their meal.

At night I became the sentry who forced the kids to sleep. Now I understood why the older girls tried so hard to get us to sleep when I was a little child there. I wanted to go upstairs and take care of my needs, not be in charge of a bunch of restless kids.

I reached my nadir when I had to supervise the playroom. My time there as a small child had created bad memories; the fighting, going to the bathroom as a group, the sheer number of kids. A club-footed boy, Georgie, who had been fitted with a heavy boot, used his boot as a weapon. He was sneaky and had to be watched every minute. I found a malleable girl who I tutored in reading to escape my anger. I became distracted working with her, until the matron told me to quiet the fighting kids. Interventions were needed constantly especially with Georgie. We would watch each other's every move and he could outfox me often and kick a child with his foot weapon. After all, I was watching 24 other kids. He knew I had no control over punishments. That was the matron's job to punish. I felt like I couldn't handle any infraction whether it be big or small from him. Finally, I got so angry at him I gave him a hard hit to his head with my hand and scared myself. I always hated fighting, and yet, I still do my share of it although infrequently.

I knew I couldn't stay at Reed any longer after I got so angry at Georgie for his misbehaving. He was constantly pulling my chain and I had had it up over the top of my head. I went to the office of the superintendent and told him what I had done and if he didn't remove me, I would kill Georgie or at least severely harm him. I was removed from playroom supervision that same day but remained in Reed cottage. I felt that as thirteen year olds we had much too much responsibility.

For six months I had the perk of cleaning two living rooms before school. I learned to "clean" a room so it looked clean without doing a thorough job. We never received newspapers, so I relished hiding with the paper and reading it while the matron and cook were eating breakfast. Dick Tracy was my favorite cartoon and I was shocked when I read the news to find that other people committed suicide besides my father. I didn't get caught with the paper but I did put it together so it looked unread.

I have been a hyper-vigilant and perceptive person all my life, a trait I developed to protect myself. On one job I had in my later years, it was a secret that the executive was going to retire. No one knew it but I reported it to my husband days before it was announced. Everyone but me was shocked when they heard him announce it. The executive was stunned when I told him I was not surprised. When he asked me how I knew, I couldn't answer and still can't. My feelings have always been intense and I pick up on little innuendos all the time. I could feel when the bullies would attack and brace myself for the abuse I saw would occur. I was right almost always. In therapy years later, one of my psychiatrists asked me how I got to the fourth floor while the psychiatrist was still in the basement because I had told him that a mutual friend had an anger problem. He agreed but never suspected it before I pointed it out to him.

Today if I feel unseen or unheard in any conversation. I will cut my sentence in midstream rather than be ignored or I will go off the subject to test their awareness. Those folks do not become friends or acquaintances.

I was supervising a group of kids making their heapys one day when I had to go to the staff bathroom. I saw blood on my underpants and decided to remain calm and bleed to death quietly and alone. I told no one but I most certainly was petrified about dying so young. How naïve I was! A few days later my roommate found me out and explained why I had to tell the nasty matron. She told me nothing but equipped me with the bulky pads. My coworker explained things to me. I was a late bloomer as a fourteen year old.

I was sent to the fourth floor of Santee, finally understanding why I had never been sent there before. I had less stress there than during all my years at Bethany. My wish was to get to high school and meet the "townies" and see happy kids with happy families. Until now, except for group trips, we were isolated from the rest of the world. Now, I would be going "out there" in the fall. It probably helped give me the impetus and strength to leave Mr. Stoltzfus because I knew that somewhere out there it would be better and I would finally be out in the world.

My tormenters were now in Moyer Cottage, where the oldest girls lived. Margie and I were going there together because we were going to ninth grade high school off campus. Since a few were seniors, I knew when I got there that some of my tormentors would either be gone or close to leaving Bethany. That included the ring leader. Although Margie was a friend, we ran into some hard times as all friends do. We would get so angry with each other that we would stop talking as Pennsylvania Dutch often do. I would be crushed, but we were both so proud that sometimes we didn't talk for what felt like ages. I would miss her but was too proud to take the first step toward reconciliation. One time our conflict was resolved when Margie made sure I overheard her tell someone I had pretty eyes. Another time we resolved things when I told her to be careful when she went outside, because I had just seen a snake. That is another Pennsylvania Dutch custom to address something other than the real issue if it is emotionally charged.

One time when she was at her dad's house she dated my ex-boyfriend, who I still felt passionate about. She immediately asked me when she got home: "Is it okay that I dated Jimmy while I was home?" Since I was no longer his girlfriend, I told her it was fine.

She didn't need me to sanction the date, as he was through with me. It did hurt, but the friendship was more important.

My eighth grade graduation was fast approaching. It was 1943. We were primed to answer questions posed by the superintendent of schools. The question I most remember was the population of the United States—138 million as opposed to approximately 320 million today. All of his expectations were met. We listened respectfully as the superintendent gave us our graduation address. We barely knew the man and yet he seemed to have such power over us.

Graduation was panic time. I would have to leave Mr. Stoltzfus and returning to visit him was a taboo. On our last day he gave us a farewell speech in his usual quiet and calm manner. I lingered to be the last one to leave. We gave each other a Pennsylvania Dutch goodbye—smiling faces and no tears. Hugs were not routine with him, but I got one last one. For the first time I instinctively hugged him back and was afraid I would cry so I held on to him beyond what was a normal goodbye. He released me and I was gone. I walked away from him forever, although I didn't know then that it would be forever.

Chapter Eight

MOYER WAS THE LOVELIEST of all the campus buildings with a cozy front porch with half a dozen antique chairs. It felt good just to look at the building. You entered a beautiful well-furnished living room with a big inviting fireplace and a small balcony on the second floor overlooking the living room and lovely wooden beams in the ceiling. I could still be cozy if I sat in such a delightful room. The kitchen was state of the art for the time. What a joy not to have a dormitory on the second floor but rooms for two or four girls. I was lucky. I was placed in a room for two girls with lots of windows, and kept that same room during my entire four-year stay.

Moyer Cottage

The back stairwell led to the outside door, which was our escape route because it led us up to the woods for the nights we sneaked out to town or Reading. Bethany kept every cottage in repair at all times. I could call the maintenance man in the morning and the problem was resolved when I came home from work or school. No wonder I have always maintained my residences in near perfect order.

I could choose my own hairstyles, and most of us got rid of bangs and wore long coifs. What a joy to control my own hair! We set our hair every night in the style we picked for ourselves. Since we would now be attending the high school in town, I think Bethany didn't want us to stand out as different. Up until then we had to cut our hair the Bethany style of an ugly coif cut straight across from ear to ear and bangs.

I began to critically study my figure and dress in a manner I felt could flatter me. I never was satisfied with how I looked (face or figure) because I thought I looked like my mother and that was bad; yet I couldn't change looking like her. She was not attractive to me then, but she would have been under different circumstances. The clothes I wore looked beautiful to me but not on me nor did I feel they flattered me. How could I appreciate anything that was a part of my mother? In spite of the attention I was getting from townies, I was unhappy. But again, I never showed this side in public. I didn't feel pretty and I thought my figure needed much improvement. Funny because every time I meet someone from my class or other classes, they now start the conversation with, "You were the prettiest girl in our class." I never saw myself in that light. I smiled and laughed a lot until I was alone and then all my demons came out. I felt so awfully ashamed of my mother I figured that I too was a shame and a bad person.

All the cottages got their clothes from the store room under the Administration Building, where Santee was located. Moyer girls could request whatever we wanted or manipulate to get what we wanted, and donations from UCC churches were so generous that I had seven pairs of shoes to choose from all through high school. I would tell the matron in the store room that my shoes were worn out or too tight. I was given new ones, but I also kept the old ones. We exchanged dresses with each other if we tired of our own. Womelsdorf was a small lower middle class town and we were dressed like upper middle class teenagers. The townies envied us, but I would rather have had what they had—parents.

When we entered the ninth grade (with the full size class of 28), 5 of us came from Bethany and we were better prepared for our studies than the townies. Mr. Stoltzfus had done his job well. We didn't necessarily graduate with higher grades than the townies.

We were up at 6:00 AM and had breakfast, so we could be off to finish our jobs by seven. I had to go back to Reed for a year to wash diapers. This required me to walk halfway across the campus, about a quarter of a mile. I was no longer afraid of the same Reed matron, because I hardly saw her. I cleaned the diapers, still fearful that someone was in the basement and left to get ready for school. After I finished that odious task, I rushed back to catch the 8:00 bus for school. The fast walk I did between Reed and Moyer got me the most improved girl award on an Anniversary Day. The driver didn't wait, so you had to be on time or walk a mile and a half to town. I never had to walk, except when I would sneak through the woods to ball games or to meet a boy in town to go to Speck's, which had a soda fountain and a dance floor. I often thought I wanted to become a dancer, but I never had lessons nor were they available to us. Eventually, we were caught and taken back to Bethany by the superintendent. Someone in town always ratted on us. The Bethany boys rode to school with us and criticized us as we boarded. I didn't wear bras when I needed them because I was embarrassed to ask for them until one boy said, "Go get bras, you're bouncing." Next I was told I had a "fat ass." I attempted to hide it and I still wonder whether it's too big. All this reinforced my ugliness to me.

The town kids were nice and never treated us differently because we were from Bethany. We had so much candy we would share with them. They thought we were great kids. We liked them too but I began to see that some of them were unhappy and that was surprising to me. We didn't talk to them about their families but sometimes they told us stories about each other. I learned all that looks good is not necessarily so with families.

We were on our own with homework. No more formal study hour, so we studied little. No jobs were assigned after dinner unless you had kitchen responsibilities, which I had during my junior and senior years. Those years I cooked for the whole cottage. For breakfast I cooked hot cereal, eggs, a breakfast meat, or mush. I was responsible for the clean-up crew and that could be problematic. They resented my being in charge and there were times when I had to nag with no support from the matron. She seemed to think we were there to wait on her and she took little responsibility except to issue any order that came down from the administration building.

Lunch was no fun on school days. We never had sandwiches so I had an hour and a half to cook, get the kitchen and dining room cleaned up, and get myself ready to go back to school. It took a while to get ready because I wanted to wash off all the morning pancake makeup and apply a new coat. I wore makeup to hide my awful looks. I cooked and supervised all the other kitchen staff responsibilities. I did the cooking alone because the matron couldn't cook. I had to teach myself to make dishes according to the ingredients sent from the main kitchen. I remember making many hamburger and liver dishes, with the meat supplied from our own cows but I can't remember other dishes because they varied so according to what was sent to me from the kitchen. By now we had over 300 people to feed on the whole campus, including staff. My husband appreciates that I'm a good cook and like cooking.

The bus was always there at exactly 4:00, so we could get home to our chores, which we had to finish for a five o'clock dinner.

During the summer we had fresh vegetables from our farm, and during the winter we ate what we had canned all summer. Salads, however, were unavailable in winter and our substitute was often pickled beets. (I still love them.) Springtime brought us milk that tasted like onion because the cows were grazing outside and eating the spring onions that grow in the grass. We could hardly swallow it and I love onions. Our milk was not pasteurized as it is today so the onion taste did not get filtered out.

If we were sneaking out with the town boys, I would take food with me, mostly "hairy arm cookies," until I was caught. Despite the occasional hair, the baker's baked goods were awesome, whether it was cake, bread, pie, or cookies.

We had "pussy soup" for Sunday night dinner. It consisted of stale bread, milk, cinnamon, and sugar mixed together. It was an economical meal, but we thought it was a treat. This was part of their austerity program.

During the war, churches collected and donated their ration stamps (which were for food and gas) to Bethany. Every Friday we used our own money to buy war stamps, which were stamps the government sold to support the war. We bought them at school at ten cents a stamp. Food stamps (for rationed items, like sugar) were unknown to us because Bethany shielded us from the need for them. The whole nation was sacrificing to support the troops overseas but we were kept in the dark. We continued our weekly movies, church trips, and all entertainment as if there was no war. Wouldn't it have been better for us to understand we too had to sacrifice? I guess they choose not to upset our routine.

One of our evening past times was listening to soap operas on the radio, ("Young Widow Brown") or mysteries ("Inner Sanctum") in the first floor living room. Television didn't exist back then. When mysteries got tense, we often were bombarded with toilet paper by the girls who were on the second floor balcony which overlooked the living room. They would wait for the scariest part of the story and distract us just like a bomb falling unexpectedly. Most of the girls enjoyed this, but it upset my enjoyment of the story. Ten o'clock meant "lights out." Some of the girls talked after ten but not me. I went to sleep to avoid sharing thoughts or feelings. I thought about getting old enough to leave Bethany and have a better life, and about the boys in our class who liked me. I was aware I was depressed and started to become bitter about my fate in life. I felt any child of my mother's would be a failure. I felt like I wore a sweat shirt that said I am Elsie Gensemer's daughter. Before, I drifted along from day to day but I was now conscious of my feelings of abandonment, despair, and angst. I preferred to be alone and couldn't tell Margie or the staff how badly I felt. I thought I was the only one who felt that way because no one talked about feelings not even Margie. I wanted to go to sleep and not wake up, but I didn't share any of this. The intensity of my feelings was scary. Even now it is so hard to put into words how badly I felt. The feelings were so deep and traumatic and many years after Bethany I continued to feel the same way. I could stifle them as long as I was involved in an activity, and I still do that sometimes to avoid negative feelings. You have to work through these feelings to become a mature adult. Bethany didn't have psychological help for us because the belief was tender loving care would take care of our hurts.

Three of my bullies lived at Moyer, but I wasn't too concerned. They did less bullying because I began to stand up to them. Standing up to them was easier because they were never all at the same place at the same time anymore. We worked at different places on the grounds and we all were busy with our jobs. I loved the cottage and the cooking, so I was in a more relaxed state of mind. Nevertheless, their words still hurt. The worst one worked in the superintendent's residence and was hardly at Moyer except at bedtime. By that time, I was in my room and the bully was in hers so I didn't have to see her. In retrospect, it seems the staff knew about the bullying because I was never placed close to them in Moyer. Or maybe it was just dumb luck.

One day I saw one of my bullies (the worst one) packing up to leave Bethany permanently and I kept track of her every move. I knew what I was going to say to her as she left, and that was "good riddance to bad rubbish." She answered "same to you" and was gone. I gave the same farewell to each of them. I felt relieved when I did this and I felt a tiny bit of justice had been done.

The only bully left began to chide me one morning about my poor baseball skills. I listened for a while and jumped up surprising her, and hit her. Would you believe later in life she became my obnoxious sister-in-law! I was five feet and ninety pounds, and she was much bigger and stronger, about 5'4" with huge breasts. She flailed back at me and I ducked under her humongous breasts. When she was worn out, I took her on until the recreation director (a Bethany alumnus who was a student at Ursinus University) made us quit. She called me away from the girls and all she said was, "I expected better than that from you." That was such a jolt because I heard it as a compliment, and no one had complimented me for years. Worthless was how I saw myself. This little bit of encouragement felt big and profound. I was sure I'd have to take care of myself the rest of my life, because who would ever want me or care about me? I never forgot this intervention and told her so years later.

Nevertheless, recreation was terrible for me. I really was a horrendously awful baseball player and we played it so much during the summers. I could never make a bat and ball meet. I was tormented for my lack of ability and no one wanted me on their team. I panicked about having my turn at bat and hated that damn ball. The recreation leader did her best to stop the ridicule, but to no avail.

One day, I heard my name being called desperately to the bathroom by a girl who sounded scared to death. She informed me she was not urinating but bleeding and begged me to stop the bleeding. She said she had snuck into Reading and had sex with her boyfriend, and begged me not to tell anyone. I was so afraid she would bleed to death that I immediately reported her to the matron who called the superintendent. I had to report it as I felt her life was at stake. This was the second time I broke our rule of ethics. She was taken to the infirmary and all her belongings were collected. She was expelled and we never saw her again. I didn't feel guilty because I felt I saved her life.

We were called into the living room for a meeting with the superintendent's wife about the expulsion. She focused on us "sneaking out," but didn't mention sex because sex didn't exist. She reiterated that a pregnancy would get us thrown out. I was shocked when my friend Margie told me, after we had left Bethany, that some of the girls were having sex while on campus. I couldn't believe how naïve I was. Why would I have known when I had rendered myself asexual? Somehow, kissing was not sexual.

Our next big meeting was to tell us one of the girls had been expelled because she got pregnant picking flowers in the woods. Who was she kidding—we were sixteen years old! She reiterated that pregnancy would get us expelled and she wanted no more "sneaking out." I realized what a big investment they had in our graduating, as well as in our chastity. As a result of that meeting I decided to avoid sex unless I was married. I would never do "that" and stuck by that resolve for years. Now I appreciate their devotion to all of us and their wish for us to become whatever they could help us become.

Most of the Bethany boys dropped out of school, but the girls usually graduated. At sixteen the boys could work on a farm, as did my oldest brother. I only found out years later as I wasn't even aware he was gone. I opted for graduation partly to postpone leaving Bethany but mostly because I knew the value of a diploma. The girls who didn't graduate could leave earlier and become live-in maids or nannies. That was not for me.

Some nights we would go to our dam and ice skate, and invite the town boys to meet us there. This activity was unsupervised. One night a boy from town came over and invited me to go on a bike ride with him, which I did. We never had bikes so this was an alluring gesture to go for a ride. He rode me to a bridge halfway between Bethany and town. There he attempted to rape me and told me he would push me into the stream if I did not submit. I fought him so hard and hit him over and over again pushing him away with my feet and cried until he released me. I never talked to him again even though his seat was next to mine all through high school. I didn't report him because I didn't want to get myself in trouble for being where I should not have been.

Our escape route to sneak away.

At night I would sneak out of the cottage with about five other kids, walk to town, and watch basketball at the high school because my boyfriend was on the team. We did this on foot because to hitchhike meant Bethany staff might pick us up.

Whenever a car approached, we lay down in a drainage ditch until it passed. After we finally got to school we were usually caught; I suspect school staff reported us. We would feel a tug on our clothes from the back and were told to, "Get in the car." Our punishment was extra jobs and we were severely scolded. That wasn't enough to stop our clandestine endeavors. We would put dummies in our beds or claim to have been in the bathroom or shower room if the matron found us missing from our beds. Sometimes it worked.

At the base of the campus which led to town

Sometimes we met town boys in the woods and stayed together as a group to talk. Being in a group made me feel more comfortable and less worried that we would be caught or less severely punished. One night, five of us snuck out and arranged for a car to take us to Reading. I went to see my brother, LeRoy's friends. We talked about Florida and it sounded like a Garden of Eden to me. A handsome young man who lived there told me he had lots of sensational Florida pictures he could show me. He went to a Florida resort every winter to wait on tables and I imagined him in Eden. I thought that made him quite a fancy guy, so I wasn't concerned about going up to his room alone with him and sex didn't enter my mind nor did he seem to be thinking along those lines. His pictures were everything I expected and I romanticized that I could someday be there and love it as much as he did. I didn't realize at that time that his pictures included lots of men. I considered myself undesirable and asexual so I wallowed in his happiness. After all, who would be interested in an orphan? I didn't know he was a homosexual and had I been told I wouldn't have known what that meant. I naively invited him to be my prom date at graduation; he sent a corsage but didn't show up. Margie told me he was a "queer." When I corrected her grammar, she laughed and told me what it meant. It was shocking to me. I went to the prom alone with Margie and her date, where I met my old boyfriend and danced with him most of the night. At intermission, we went to a club, the Black Duck, and I was shocked how tame it was because we were always told it was like a whorehouse. It seemed such an innocent place to me.

Two days after we snuck out, the stern scary superintendent's wife called everyone in the cottage to the living room for a meeting. She knew five of us went to Reading, but she didn't know which five. The whole cottage pleaded innocent and we thought she would give up on finding out which ones had sneaked out. The next day I was told to go to the Bowmans' home for the weekend. I hadn't seen them for years. At dinner their conversation turned to this incident and, of course, I denied any involvement. When I was driven back to Bethany, I was told to report to the superintendent's house with the Bowmans. I found the superintendent had called in the state police to get confessions from the girls. Of course, they had to mention me as one of them. I cried and begged not to be thrown out. I was told to return to Moyer and go to bed. The superintendent felt we had been punished appropriately and we thought we would never hear about it again. But for me, it wasn't over. Another brother who lived in Reading had written a letter to Bethany to report that I had gone to a man's room. Who knows what possessed him to do this. My punishment was to return to the baby cottage and have my underpants checked each night by the matron I detested, to prove to the orphanage that I was not pregnant. This was so humiliating and I resented my brother for being such a rat. I felt the matron was saying, "See, you're like your mother." When I got my period, I was returned to Moyer. Had I not gotten it I would have been expelled.

During my last two years at Moyer, I went to a church camp located in a lovely rural area, for two weeks in the summer. My cabin of ten chose me to represent them on the camp senate. These were wonderful times for me. My eczema disappeared and I got into a clique of Norristown girls and thought their town must be a magical place, as they were good friends and such caring girls. I am still in touch with one of them. These vacations boosted my ego and helped me tolerate my last years at Bethany. Years later I found out Bethany asked the Bowmans to pay the camp bill, but I never thanked them because I resented that they cared for me sporadically. I don't think they would have paid on their own. They weren't that aware of me.

The lake was icy cold, but each morning those who took a pre-breakfast dip were recognized at breakfast by the other kids and staff. I plunged into the frigid lake almost every day because I needed the kudos all the campers heaped on me and the rest of the brave souls. Camp was the first place I ever received compliments and I loved hearing them. In Bethany we followed orders and rarely heard a please or thank you. At camp I got used to saying and hearing those words. I belonged there and was ecstatic about being liked. I almost felt like a person. I cried with my friends when the two weeks were over. I dreaded going back because I would again have to face my demons which I had successfully stuffed while there. I began to make my own decisions while there because except for a few camp rules no one dictated what we could or could not do. That made going back to Bethany hard. I reverted back to the compliant child. I detested that role more than ever now that I had a taste of being able to think for myself. After all, I was a teenager yearning for independence.

My time at Moyer seemed to go so quickly. I was quite conflicted about my approaching high school graduation and leaving the home I had for fifteen and a half years. Where would I go? What would I do? Who would I depend on? Would I feel free? Most of all, would I be happy? That was what I longed for, just as my parents had. I knew someday I could be happy but I had to make it happen and I didn't know how.

We usually left Bethany at age eighteen, but for me to graduate from high school I needed to stay until I was eighteen and a half because I had flunked seventh grade. The superintendent requested that the board let me stay and they granted him permission to keep me until graduation which I am still grateful for. What a wonderful decision that was and what a relief for me, because I could not have graduated without that privilege to stay. What I couldn't articulate was the fear and trepidation I felt about leaving. None of us ever talked about these fears. Instead, we would gripe about Bethany and talk about how glad we were to leave. That was easier. I knew I had to have a decent job to attain my goals and meet people, so that fueled my desire for a high school diploma.

A few days before graduation, we five grads were driven to Lebanon to shop for clothing, a suitcase, and toiletries, in preparation for our new life. We were allowed to pick our own items, although we had to stay within a certain price range and my choices were gorgeous in my eyes. I never heard of another orphanage that did this for graduates. I am grateful to Bethany for this privilege as it left me with the feeling I could move on. Bethany does not do this today. It is no longer a home to kids, but like many residential placements merely a temporary stop.

The institution is never a placement long enough to allow bonds to form. I feel this approach is wrong because too many kids have multiple placements now but no real home. Bethany became so much like home to me that I couldn't accept breaking that bond to become adopted. When adoption was presented to me, I was already bonded to both Miss Anna and Mr. Stoltzfus. I couldn't leave them.

They are often returned to homes who can't provide for them. I remember sending a child home to a mother who was living in a small one room in a house with only a small fireplace to keep warm. She also had two other little children. She apparently believed that the son who was returned to her could get work to help pay the bills. He had no training for any trade nor the mental capacity to do what needed to be done to salvage the family. I think the negative bonding that occurs and holds kids to their parents after they are placed, needs to be acknowledged and worked through. Children need more understanding of why their home will not let them have life growing experiences that will give them the ability to move on with their lives in their later years. Often because families can't afford transportation, these children no longer receive services they require. Institutions are so frowned upon today and it is not the institution vs. the home that is the issue, but rather the quality of care given to the kids no matter the setting.

From fifth through twelfth grade while going to school, I was the dental assistant every Friday. I had to make up any school work I missed and I could not choose one over the other. Doing both was a non-negotiable expectation of me. I never thought about whether I liked the job or not. I just did it. This was the beginning of a later career for me.

About a week before I was to leave, I was driven to the Reading YWCA to see the little room where I would live. A half block away was the dental office where I would work. I was never interviewed by anyone in the office nor did I meet the dentist before my first day at work. Bethany interviewed him without me. A restaurant was pointed out to me and that was where I was told I would eat. I was exhilarated about having a new life, but also scared and worried. Some of my biological relatives lived in Reading and I felt I could visit them if I was lonely; I anticipated some loneliness. I didn't know where they lived, but knew I could find them if I wanted to visit. I wonder why Bethany didn't try to connect us.

Graduation was wonderful. I felt so excited and my cap and gown made me feel like I had some meaning. After the exercises we had a dance in town and Bethany didn't supervise us nor did they set a curfew. I felt free already. That night was magical. It was all about my present feelings and the future just had to wait. I had no apprehensions because I danced with my high school sweetheart most of the night. He mesmerized me and promised we would be together after Bethany. I was so in love and he loved me! My joy was indescribable. The words to one of the songs we danced to spoke to me as they were my feelings completely:

It was just a neighborhood dance.
That's all that it was
But oh what it seemed to be.

This song described all my joys such as Anniversary Day or Hershey. They were always more than I could imagine and so magical.

I didn't think to say goodbye to Miss Anna or Mr. Stoltzfus, nor were we encouraged to do so. I still regret that I didn't just do it. I didn't say goodbye to my two younger brothers either, but they were probably unaware of my leaving. No one encouraged goodbyes. My exhilaration about the future faded when I finally left Bethany. Now I was terrified and loneliness set in right away. How could I live with twenty-five girls for over fifteen years on a huge campus, and then live alone in a single room? I felt overwhelmed with grief and terror.

Who was I at age eighteen and a half? I had no idea nor did I belong to anyone or have a real home. When I was around other people, I was able to bury the psychological pain I had endured but continued to feel all the negative feelings secretly. I was able to stuff my depression and pretend to be happy. I wore a smile on my face most of the time. What else could I do? There was no one to understand me or to help me so smiling seemed better than facing my pain and sadness. That was the survival mechanism I learned at Bethany. But when I was alone, all the hurts and insecurities returned in spades. Yet at the same time, on some level, my spirit and optimism were intact.

On that last day, I went to the treasurer to get my bank account closed out. When he gave me $50, I was shocked. I had expected a minimum of $300. I had saved $5 every Anniversary Day. I had saved every dollar I got from cleaning the teacher's room. I saved the money my oldest brother sent me every year for Christmas. I saved every nickel the doctor had given me for spotting a bluebird. I saved the $50 I got for being the most improved girl one year. I questioned the treasurer, but he said the bank had my book so he couldn't show it to me to prove he was accurate. I suspected he stole the money, but I didn't tell him what I thought. These suspicions were confirmed when other classmates had the same experience. How could he live with himself? He was the same man who used me as a flower girl when he got married. He has died so he will never face his theft nor be held accountable.

It was June 1949, and the big day had finally arrived. My last act was to tell my last bully "good riddance" and I was out the door. No one was there to say goodbye and wish the best for me, not even the matron of the cottage. The superintendent's daughter (the same one that was the recreational director) drove me to Reading and without turning the ignition off, she dropped me at the front door of the Y and was gone. I got out, took my things, went into the Y alone. I felt like a cow being lead to a slaughter. I was accustomed to a lovely campus and beautiful ambience and all I had now was a small room. I wanted so much to have a mother who could tell me I would be all right and help me sort out what I was doing for the rest of my life. I yearned for parents all my time at Bethany, but now I needed them more than ever. I had to face the fact that I would never have them. I was too depressed and sad to go out for the rest of the day. I was apprehensive about going to the restaurant, so I went to sleep without dinner. I wanted to do well on the job and feared meeting my boss. What a mess I was!

Chapter Nine

THE REALITY OF BEING on my own was daunting and chilling, but I was determined to live up to my mantra: *don't be like your mother*. The fact that I would be like my immoral mother was thrown in my face so often, I lived each day to prove to myself I would not be like her. I was determined to find my own happiness no matter what I had to do to achieve this. I would take advantage of any opportunity that came my way. Would I like my boss? Would he like me? I had my school guidance counselor's words to spur me on: "You are college material." I felt if I were really college material then I could handle being a dental assistant. I thought my problems would diminish once I was working. No such luck! I went to the assigned breakfast with great trepidation and ate at the counter. I got to know the lovely waitress well after a few weeks and we talked a lot, but she committed suicide with her married boyfriend not long after we were had established a relationship. My expectation was that she would be my new mother. Her death grieved me for a long time, as she was my first acquaintance after Bethany and again I had no one to talk to. With great apprehension, I showed up on the doorstep of the dental office.

    The dentist was a short Jewish man who introduced himself and showed me his five-room dental office. I had never seen more than a tiny one-room office and was impressed. His kind secretary was a married middle-aged woman who was helpful when I ran into snags. My boss was a perfectionist and I never learned to relax in his office because of his two personalities. In the office he was an authoritarian who could reduce me to tears. At 5:00 PM, he became this wonderful man who took me to his home for dinner with his family or to Galen Hall, a resort located in Wernersville. Every month he took his staff to the elegant Abraham Lincoln Hotel for lunch. It was the second best restaurant in Reading and I was totally enchanted to be there. It is now being renovated to its previous elegance, and my husband and I eat there when we visit my brother even though the food leaves a lot to be desired. I watched my boss to learn proper eating etiquette and what new foods to try. Would you believe I had never eaten tuna or peanut butter! Our Bethany food was whatever they could raise.

I requested free dancing lessons from the Y but was turned down, so my boss arranged free lessons at the Jewish Y and I took them. I began to look for new lodgings because the Y imposed a 9:00 curfew but I moved four times that year before I settled down in a room with wonderful college graduate women who shared the house with me and "adopted" me. They helped me adjust to the big world and to my living situation. How fortuitous and fruitful! They often cooked a free dinner for me and talked to me about going to college. I listened, but it sounded like a dream I could never fulfill. I knew I could be happy living in a dorm, but could I do the work required? I had mixed emotions about going but didn't rule it out as a possibility.

I found it difficult to occupy myself after work. What to do? Where to go? What did I want? I couldn't answer those questions, so many nights I walked Penn Street, the main drag, and people watched or window shopped. I watched people come and go from the Crystal Restaurant, Reading's most popular and best. I wondered how anyone could afford to eat there, especially the seafood. I had never eaten seafood, but my office friends made my mouth drool when they told me about it. I envied those who could afford it. In retrospect it was not that expensive, but I couldn't afford it on my small salary.

Occasionally, I passed my mother on the street and I would feel a tug at my heart thinking she could be a resource for me but I immediately tossed that idea aside as it was a pipedream and I knew it. We both recognized each other, but I was too angry and ashamed to acknowledge her and just kept walking. She never attempted to stop me. She wore the same depressed look and the horrible housedresses I hated so much. She looked pitiful to me and I was ashamed of her. How I yearned for a mother, but not that one. In fact, I had rejected her 100%. Did she care that I snubbed her? I never knew.

LeRoy, my second oldest brother, who left Bethany years before me, had me over for dinner once I learned how to get to his apartment. I remain grateful to him for this act of kindness. I didn't have money, and although he had a lot of kids and was struggling financially, he fed me with no hesitation and often. Even during my college years, he would invite me to stay at his place and fed me as well. I had no contact with my oldest brother, who was married and also living in Reading.

One landlady had a blind veteran friend. She requested I date him and I agreed, He was very authoritarian and I turned him down after one date. Then I was asked to go to the Valley Forge Military Hospital on a weekly basis to dance with wounded veterans. I went a few times, but found my partners to be as lonely as I was, which made them too aggressive for me. I became a regular at the library and used reading as an excuse to stay in my room. I was anything but happy. What would become of me?

I worried about dying and ending up in a pauper's grave, which I thought would be my mother's fate although thankfully it wasn't. So I took out a life insurance policy that matured at $1,000 and I paid $1 a week for the inner peace it brought. This made me feel I was on my way to succeeding.

I lived briefly in a room in Mt. Penn. At the top of the hill was a hangout for college kids. A friend took me there and introduced me to a young sophomore college boy. He would stay and dance with me all evening and tell me fraternity stories. I was an enchanted audience and wallowed in his tales. When he went back to school, we sent letters back and forth, and he promised to date me when he came home. When he returned, he sought me out and we took a ride that ended in a deserted pasture. Then he tried to rape me. I fought hard, hitting him, biting him, and begging him to stop. He was extremely aggressive I felt lucky to get away. It was a close call. I told him I hated him. He finally let me go and I never heard from him again nor did I go back to that hangout. I lost some of my adoration of college people. I told my boss about the incident, but the man's father was a big storeowner on Penn St. and a friend of my boss, so my boss never told me that I should go to the police. He did tell me that I was more vulnerable than girls with parents to support them and men knew I had no one to report to. I resented that it was true, but I never forgot what he said.

The secretary at the office was replaced by a lovely young Jewish woman. She and my boss talked a lot about cultural things, like concerts and plays. I couldn't afford the arts and craved those privileges. I learned to respect and adore Jewish people and still have many Jewish friends. She was constantly talking to me about going to dental hygiene school, but I turned a deaf ear to her. I owe her a big thank you also but I've lost touch with her.

The last place I roomed with my two college friends was the home of a Jewish social worker near Albright College. I started to hang around the college's sports arenas to watch practices because I thought I might meet some college men. At the tennis stadium I met three charming lovely sisters who played tennis every week and befriended me. This gave me the impetus to hang out with them every Saturday when the courts filled up. They introduced me to Ted, a Lehigh University tennis player who lived across the street from my room. He asked to pick me up at my office for a dinner date the following Monday. I accepted and was thrilled to accept his invitation and we commenced to date all summer. We went to clubs, the Reading Country Club, Sunnybrook where the big bands of the '50s played, listened to Vaughan Monroe radio shows, and ate in wonderful restaurants. I thought he was wonderful and enjoyed his company tremendously. He was special and I learned a lot of etiquette from him—not because he taught me directly, but because I am a good observer.

One night I went on a cruise to the West Point Academy in upstate New York with a high school friend. I was so impressed with the aura of learning and enlightenment that I began listening to the voices telling me I could make it in college. When I got back, I was determined to go to Temple University School of Oral Hygiene in Philadelphia. Even the big city intrigued me. I was beyond excited to think that I might get into a college and I had four people rooting for me—my two roommates, the secretary at the office, and myself. I applied without telling anyone except my two friends in the house, not even my boss or Ted.

I submitted my Temple application and the Bethany board members approved an interest free loan. I heard from Temple very quickly because someone had dropped out for that fall. I was just three months short of twenty and on cloud nine. The school's assistant supervisor lived in Reading; she came to interview me and I was accepted. I couldn't wait to shout this acceptance to the world, but I dreaded telling my boss who had been so good to me outside of the office. I can still see the shocked look on his face. He asked me why I hadn't told him I was applying. I was so frightened that I told him it was Bethany's idea. I gave him a few weeks' notice and it calmed him down. It was comforting to know that he must have liked my work, because he was disappointed I was leaving.

Ted and I were a couple by then but we never discussed our feelings. He was very important and attractive to me. I feared he would forget me if I moved to Philadelphia. I never found out if he knew about my history. We never visited each other in our homes, although we lived across the street from each other. I never told him about Bethany because I never got over the inferior feelings I had about being an orphan. I believed that would have been the kiss of death for me.

One morning while I was living at the social worker's home, I dressed sloppily and wore no makeup to walk half a block to pick up cereal. When I got back, my landlady told me never to do that again because "all you have going for you is your body." It hurt, and worst of all I believed her!

Ted was so respectful of me. He seemed to care for me, was such a gentleman, and never took me for granted. My few years with him were wonderful. No one had ever opened a car door for me before. He was a quiet and shy kind of guy, but treated me like a princess. Who would not have loved that kind of attention!

My roommates insisted I needed clothes and should tap into my savings account to buy them. I didn't want to spend savings for which I had worked so hard. I was proud of the fact that I had saved, but the girls reassured me that after college I would be able to save again. I had given up many lunches to save and that money was my security. Reluctantly, I gave in and we shopped. One of them took me shopping for an evening gown (which I thought I would never use), a suit, blouse, shoes, and two dresses. I was shocked at how far my savings went. Little did I know that I would end up with three evening gowns during my two years at Temple University School of Dental Oral Hygiene. They were so right about my needs and I wish I could thank them, but a few months after school started I lost contact with them. I rue the day I let that happen.

Ted left for college before I did. We said goodbye and I thought we were over, but how wrong I was. I went to Lehigh to watch him play tennis and attend exciting fraternity parties for another two years. We never did discuss feelings so neither of us knew whether the other was serious about the relationship or not.

In the summer I told the Bowmans that I was going to college in the fall and they offered to take me to Philadelphia. I went to their house for Christmas that year on my birthday. They didn't acknowledge my birthday, but I didn't expect it either as I had never had a birthday party my entire life. I didn't realize that celebrating birthdays is a custom for families. Later in my life, some of my friends had birthday parties for me. With great trepidation, fear, and excitement, I accepted the Bowmans offer of a ride and I was off to Temple University School of Oral Hygiene.

Chapter Ten

I WAS THE LAST STUDENT to arrive in the afternoon. Because the dorm was full, five freshmen dental hygiene students and I were staying in a Jewish sorority house next to Mitten Hall, a center for Temple activities. The Bowmans left almost immediately. To avoid telling my awful life story, I explained why my last name was different from the Bowmans by saying that Mr. Bowman wasn't my father. I didn't explain that Mrs. Bowman wasn't my mother. That explanation lasted for my two years at Temple. I was too ashamed to tell them about the orphanage. It was almost like everyone in the world had parents except me.

Our chaperone lived on the second floor and the six of us were on the third. My room was the only single, which I preferred. I was there to further my career and meet college men. I couldn't wait to date.

I felt inferior because I believed all the other girls had caring loving parents and were happy people. Of course, that was a fantasy. The first few weeks I made many calls to Reading to the two college graduates and the three sisters I met at the tennis stadium. These calls decreased over time when I found my classmates accepted me, and I became busy dating and going to school. I was about to embark on two of the best years of my life. I am so grateful for those years and for every opportunity they afforded me to transform into a new person. I became outgoing and stood up to obnoxious men who thought they could take advantage of me.

Our class was comprised of forty-eight girls and we held all our classes in the dental school. We never mixed with other students from the university. Dental hygiene was a relatively new field and we were told how special we were, including, they said, being better than nurses. Even though I knew it wasn't true, this helped my ego. We were assigned seats alphabetically and kept the same seat for two years. I am still in touch with the girls on either side of me.

After lunch we sat in the lobby. The dental and pharmacy students walked through and we checked out everyone that walked through to see if they were possible dates and the students looked us over also. Some classmates married these students, but I wasn't into getting married as I was having too much fun. Fraternity parties were new to me and I wanted to be included in all of them but that was a dream. There were too many. I was able to handle dates and school, and I manipulated my grades so I wouldn't flunk out. Obviously, I could never be an honor student. I dated students who were gentlemen and respected me like Ted, who I was still seeing most weekends. I had so much respect for him that I would forego any other weekend invitations.

Ted hitchhiked to Reading from Bethlehem many Wednesday nights, picked up his father's car, then came to Temple to take me to dinner, and reversed the routine to get back to Lehigh. That was about an hour and a half one way. I enjoyed all my time with him and especially the Lehigh weekend parties. I almost feel my alma mater was Lehigh, as Fred, my future husband, also graduated from there.

One of the six girls who lived with me, met a psychology student next door and they went to dinner each night. Soon another boy joined them and I did too. They were New Yorkers and so much fun. For the whole year I was happy eating with only the four of us. It was great company and good conversation. I adored my friend and felt guilty when he flunked out of pre-dental school, because I had talked to him until bedtime many nights. Our rooms were across from each other in a space between our two buildings. We sat on our window sills and chatted away. I loved this time with him. I felt relieved to know he eventually became a dentist. We lost track of each other and what a gift it would be to talk with him again. I remember one naïve conversation I had with him. I insisted that Mario Lanza was a better singer than Caruso. When I went to the Academy of Music to hear Mario, I couldn't convince him to go with me. What a disappointment.

Life was fun for me every day. No bullies. Good friends. School was manageable and I was having lots of dates. I denied my past, told no one about it, and was glad to bury it. Little did I understand it would come back to haunt me years later. But for now, life was wonderful. I don't believe I was ever depressed during those two years.

Vacations were spent at the Bowmans (these were boring but I had no other place to go) or at my brother's home if I was going to date Ted. Summers I worked at the Harrisburg State Hospital for mental patients while staying at the Bowmans. At the Bowmans I dated dental students from the area. One attempted to rape me in their house. The Bowmans told me later that they heard me fighting him off and did nothing to help me. I didn't even like him so I really got loud with him and tore at his clothes to get him off of me. My date's father was a dentist, so Bowmans thought if we got serious about each other it would be wonderful. Not a chance before or after that experience.

Another time, an 85-year-old friend of the Bowmans wanted me as his Canasta partner. He made indecent passes at me in the Bowmans car as they drove us to the house where we would play. They saw me fight him off in the rearview mirror but did not intervene. Later they bawled me out for not submitting because he was wealthy and would have paid off my debts. I was in a rage and I disliked them more intensely after these horrible experiences, but I continued the relationship because I still needed a place to go during school breaks.

They were active in their church and I had to go with them when I was visiting or so they said and I was somewhat of a compliant person because I needed one of their beds as a place to stay. They were critical of the minister, a Bethany alumnus who would eventually perform my wedding ceremony. They felt he was a cold person and made bad decisions for the church, but I can't remember the details because I wasn't interested. They played a role in my becoming agnostic years later. They were considered good Christians because they went to church every Sunday. I didn't see things that way.

My second year at college was a continuation of my first, except that now all dental hygiene students lived in a separate dorm. I felt I was back at Bethany again living with about thirty girls. The rest of the girls were commuters, only this time I felt safe and secure. My friends were there.

In exchange for free room and board at the dorm, I was required to work with three World War II veteran dental students, a classmate, and a cook. We set up for dinner and cleaned up afterwards. One of the veteran students made the comment, "There are no queens in this dorm." I was so angry at him (my continual rage was always close to the surface.) I ran upstairs to our class president to report him. She spoke to him about it and they have been married at least 60 years. He found his queen.

The other veteran dental student, who worked in the dorm dated me and I fell so hard for him. One night I had a few too many drinks because he was late coming to his fraternity party and I feared he had stood me up. By the time he arrived, my classmates had hung me by my sweatshirt on the bathroom door. He took me down and put me on a bed because I was sick as a dog. He took me home and asked me for breakfast the next morning. I was so excited because he had been such a gentleman that night and I loved him for not taking advantage of me. We had breakfast and he told me he was terminating our relationship because I was too serious. My world tumbled! I continued to date others but could not forget him for years. We worked together in the kitchen, and occasionally he would back me into the pots and pans room and kiss me. I melted each time, but dates never followed.

Ted and I had been dating for four years now. I watched his tennis matches and partied with him until on one occasion he made a pass at me. I freaked out. Now I can laugh about it, but back then I couldn't because I still considered myself asexual. He ended our relationship without telling me. He just stopped calling and I was crushed. Margie from Bethany was at Cedar Crest College in Allentown. We made a pact that we would get a date for each other. I got her a date with a dental student and she got me one from Lehigh. I wanted Ted to know that I had a Lehigh date so I had Fred take me to his fraternity. I saw him with another girl and he was not at all happy to see me and that hurt.

My blind date was a shy quiet Fred Arnold—a junior. We went to his fraternity for a party and then he took me back to Cedar Crest for the night. When I got out of the car, he backed me up against a wall and kissed me. I was stunned because he had been shy all evening. This seemed so bold but nice to me. Years later he told me he did it because he figured he would never see me again.

I continued dating at the Temple dental fraternity where the love of my life, the veteran dental student, was a member. He would always tell my dates, "You got her a good girl and leave her that way." How that hurt, because I was ready to lose my reputation for him, but he never dated me again. He always thought I looked so pretty in pink. I would wear it any time he was in the dorm kitchen, but to no avail.

Fred would come to Philadelphia every Monday night for Army Reserve meetings. He would call me and we would talk (mostly laugh) for about a half hour on the telephone. He had such a good sense of humor. I seemed to attract men who didn't talk about their feelings. Fred didn't, nor did I. I was having such a good time and was sublimely happy; I didn't give my background a serious thought. I liked the variety of guys I was dating. I still felt inferior to everyone but didn't disclose those feelings. I never would display nor recognize my internal rage. Life was perfect and I thought it would stay that way forever after I graduated. I sure was in denial!

One night, my clique of classmates left the dorm without me. I was crushed. They felt like family to me. They later explained that they were going to the home of a clinical instructor who didn't like me, because I dated a dental student when I was at Bowmans who had just broken up with her. Because they didn't explain their actions before they left, I wouldn't speak to them. We all had to give speeches in public speaking class the next day. My speech was on the Pennsylvania Dutch custom of bundling—when a couple is serious but not married, they sleep in the same bed with a board between them to prevent any hanky panky. I got up to give my talk, but was so upset with my friends that I started to cry and ran out of the room. At this point in my life I was a little paranoid about people and still suppressing my childhood rage. Because my friends had snubbed me the day before, I envisioned them all laughing at me, especially the one who sat next to me. I liked her the best and hated when she was angry at me. The professor gave me an A because I tried and was well prepared. I was forever grateful to him for that. I later learned that my friends were not laughing at me. They didn't like my silence any more than I did. Not talking to someone you are mad at is Pennsylvania Dutch. It never resolves anything for either party.

Graduation was nearing and I was scared my life would be what it was in Reading. I never expressed these feelings to anyone. I wanted to cling to each girl in the clique. It was agony to feel I was being abandoned again and those feelings were becoming all pervasive but I was still smiling through my pain.

At graduation I wanted to cry but no one else did, so I kept my feelings to myself. Bethany's treasurer drove down for the occasion but remained in the background so as not to embarrass me. At the luncheon after the services I was so full of emotion. I felt angry, lost, and alone, but I swallowed all my feelings not realizing one cannot stifle them forever. They will come out whether you want them to or not even if ass backwards. I didn't know then that I was not being abandoned. In fact, I am still in touch with three girls from the clique today. I didn't realize that these feelings of abandonment came from my past history.

My dental hygiene graduation picture, 1952.

I had no plans nor did I have a job, but fortunately one of my classmates asked me to rent with her for the summer as she was getting married in September. We sublet from two women so I needed another place to stay before September. Barbara and I were not very compatible. I was neat and she was sloppy, but it was just a summer arrangement and I did find a job within walking distance. In September I moved to an apartment with two nurses. I was still dating Fred and the high school sweetheart whom I danced with at our graduation. The dental students I dated were graduated when I was.

It didn't take me long to realize that I was on a career path I didn't care to pursue. The work was routine and I got sick of talking about proper tooth care when no one wanted to hear it. I changed dental offices a few times for more money, but inside my life was in turmoil. I had already started to pay off my debt and that was the only good part of my life. I felt I had no home or family and my social life was not as full; what would the future hold for me?

I wanted to be happier. How could I make that happen? I was twenty-one and felt it was time to get my life together, but how? I had no direction or plans. I thought of going into military service or to a new town. I got a job offer from a dentist in Washington, D.C. but was afraid to move from Philadelphia where I had friends. What was to become of me? I was depressed, but had no idea about how to resolve it. I had no one I wanted to talk to about my situation. I thought I could handle it all by myself, but that wasn't working either.

That summer Fred was not around weekends because his parents had a home at the shore, and my high school sweetheart, whom I loved and planned to marry, was cheating with other women and had a dishonorable discharge from the service. That relationship ended, which added to my insecurities. I felt so alone and welcomed any distraction, even jury duty sounded exciting when I got assigned to serve. I could fake happiness if I wasn't alone, but I had no idea how to help myself except to keep on putting one foot in front of the other. I drifted along like this for a few years, but the depression never lifted. I was just existing.

Chapter Eleven

FRED GOT BACK FROM HIS weekends at the shore and continued to live with his parents in Wyncote, Pa. He would come to my apartment most nights around dinner and stay until two or three a.m. We would laugh away that whole time. I was having a wonderful time with him but like most of my dates, I didn't know what he thought of me. I assumed that anyone who had parents wouldn't marry an orphan, but I knew I was getting serious. We went out for hamburgers and cokes many nights because neither of us had any money. He was saving for a car and I was paying off my debt. Fortunately, he had no school or other debts.

One night he told me to get dressed up the following Saturday because he wanted to splurge with me. Saturday came and he called a cab to take us to Victor's Café in South Philadelphia, where the waiters and waitresses ring a bell, everyone gets quiet, and they sing arias from various operas. We still eat there occasionally. After dinner we took a cab to Sciolla's Club in North Philadelphia to listen to the Treniers and then took a cab back to my apartment. I was so touched and thrilled that someone would treat me like such a princess and I thanked him profusely. I was so naïve that I never felt any affection he may have had for me. He must have felt something positive. How did I not see it?

I couldn't continue staying up that late every night and still be effective on my job. I decided to tell Fred I loved him, and that if he didn't feel the same about me he should go home.

I needed words because I didn't see his loving actions. He got up, went home, and didn't call for two weeks. My roommate insisted that I call him but that wasn't done in those days and neither did I feel it was up to me. The ball was in his court. When he finally called, I invited him to come over. He was shy but he told me he loved me too. I wore his fraternity pin because he couldn't afford a ring, but we were committed. Now my depression was nominal.

I became more aware of my anger problem as I recognized it surfacing in my work. I hated dental hygiene and how little we got paid in those days, but felt trapped in it. I began to get snappy with bosses or anyone who I felt slighted or hurt me. I was often misinterpreting much of what was said to me. I was (and still am) too sensitive. I thought other people were out to get me because that was what I knew from Bethany

I began an innovative dental hygiene career that gave me more money and more flexibility. Instead of a full time job, I filled in at any dental office in the Philadelphia area where a hygienist was vacationing or sick. I insisted on a full schedule and a commission rather than a salary. Commissions were generally not given but they generated more income for me so I could now afford to pay off my debt. Hygienists were scarce back in 1953. My extra earnings went to pay off my debt. I liked this arrangement because if I didn't like the dentist or the office I was out of there in two weeks. Making my own decisions was necessary but I liked that responsibility rather having people tell me what to do.

In the fall of 1953, Uncle Sam called Fred to join the Army as a corporal, and he had to report to Aberdeen Proving Grounds in Maryland. When he left the service, a year later, he was a sergeant. A fellow corporal also had a girlfriend in Philadelphia. He had an old De Soto that Fred and he drove from Maryland to Philadelphia once a week to visit us for a few hours. If that wasn't a loving trip, then what else could it be! I didn't feel bad when I was with Fred, so he never saw the depressed side of me. I was deliriously happy with him and we were still laughing much of our time together.

I spent every Sunday in Maryland with him. One weekend I missed my train due to an unexpected change in schedule. This was during the Korean War. The stationmaster listened to my sad story and discovered I was going to Aberdeen to see a serviceman. He arranged to have an unscheduled train stop for me. As I boarded, the conductor welcomed me by telling the passengers in my car that I was "Miss Aberdeen." The passengers seemed to enjoy the whole deal. I felt special but also embarrassed because someone was recognizing me, a new experience except during dates. Recognition can still make me feel shy.

Fred was scheduled to go to Korea. This terrified me and we decided to get married. I was ecstatic because I felt sincerely loved. We told the Bowmans we wanted to marry. All through college I had pretended that they were my parents so I didn't have to talk about the orphanage. I felt compelled to tell them about wanting to marry. I felt they could at least pay for the wedding after all the grief they had given me. Instead, the Bowmans lived up to their horrible reputation.

They took it as their responsibility to write Fred's parents (behind my back) about their opposition to the marriage because I had a debt. Fred's parents invited me to dinner. I had not met them and didn't know about the Bowmans' letter to them, so I was delighted to go. They wanted to meet Fred's fiancée and I thought that was a lovely gesture. I heard it as a compliment. I had no inkling about what was to occur. All went well until dessert, when I was confronted with Bowmans' letter. My future-father-in-law dropped his bomb by asking me about my debt and asked me how I intended to pay it back. I told him I would work after we were married just as I was now. The next question and my anger was full blown. He asked if I was marrying Fred for his money. I told them that I did owe the money, which amounted to $1,735 at that time (about $15,000 in today's money) but that it was not his business but Fred's and mine. Bethany set no timetable for repayment, and it was an interest free loan that most alumni borrowers never repaid. During the interrogation Fred's mother remained silent. I burst into tears and told him my debt "was none of his business."

I told him that was between Fred and myself. Fred knew what I owed and didn't care. At that time Fred had just enough money to buy a used car, hardly giving me reason to think he had money. I didn't tell his dad that I had an insurance policy and a savings account for my own security. I got up and stomped out of the front door. I called Fred, and told him what transpired. He was shocked and said, "Bert, no one talks up to my father." "If I did it once," I replied, "then I can do it again if I must." My dreams of having a caring family were shattered. But this time I was not alone—I had Fred on my side. He also thought his father had no right to treat me that way nor did he think my debt was his dad's business.

My father-in-law was born in 1895. He was a thin, 5'9" man with a stern severe looking face, sharp facial features, and an equally sharp tongue. I can still see him with that smirk on his face he used behind peoples back after he had made his zinger remark. How ugly that was to me. He was musically talented and played tennis well. He had to quit school in the sixth grade to work, because his father had died when he was five and his mother had three boys and two girls to support. She was eking out a living by cleaning houses and needed the extra income. This experience and the Depression accounted for his personality. I eventually learned to respect him and like him but could not bring myself to love him nor could I communicate with him until the time of his illness and death but I am getting ahead of my story. He often misinterpreted what I would say as did Fred's oldest brother.

Fred was the youngest of three boys and born during the Depression as I was. His siblings were six and eight years older than Fred. I always kidded Fred that he was an afterthought. My mother-in-law once told me the Depression impacted them very little, even when her husband had his salary cut in half, because they lived so frugally. My future father-in-law began as an errand boy for a brokerage firm, and ended his career as a manager of Brown Brothers Harriman, a private bank and brokerage firm.

My relationship with Fred's father continued to be rocky for most of his life but when I was 54, Fred's aunt insulted our daughter one day at the shore. She went outside to avoid my screaming at her. I flew into her with words that weren't very ladylike. My father-in-law came out of his apartment in the same building to try to help but I was too angry to be shut up. He came to my defense, and that was the closest we were until he was on his deathbed in 1984 at age 89.

Fred's mother was a slightly stocky 5'4" woman who seemed to smile through the inner hurts she had suffered all through her marriage. They fought constantly and had the same argument every Sunday morning. He wanted to buy one newspaper and she wanted a different one. Although he could well afford two, he bought only one and it was his choice not hers. I witnessed this battle escalate one Sunday to terrible heights, until I thought it would lead to divorce. I was now living with Fred's parents while Fred was in the service because Fred was concerned about my safety living in North Philadelphia. He had requested that they take me in and I agreed for Fred's sake. I called Fred at the army base and told him about their argument. "Don't worry, Bert," he said, "that's their usual Sunday morning argument." It seems Fred's father couldn't handle close relationships and was an ace at distancing people. Apparently, his wife chose to suffer with him.

My mother-in-law, Ruth, had a lovely voice and sang in the local Presbyterian Church. She belonged to a woman's club in Philadelphia called The Century Club and to the Women's Civic Club in Stone Harbor, New Jersey where they had a summer home. These were her outlets. Years after her death at age 62, Fred's father told Fred and me that he "wasn't good to Ruth." I attempted to appease him, but he reiterated his truth. I let the conversation drop to avoid hurting him. All I could have said honestly was that I agreed with him. He never brought it up again.

The Arnold family couldn't deal with feelings. I was outspoken about what I thought and this made it hard for them to accept me.

With our marriage being blocked by the Bowmans and Arnolds, we eloped and married in a Presbyterian Church in Bel Air, Maryland on February 6, 1954. We were 24, although I'm three weeks older than Fred. Fred likes to needle me by saying he married an "older woman." We had a one-night honeymoon in the lovely Tuckaway Motel in Aberdeen. What a wonderful weekend that was. On Monday we went back to our respective jobs and my worries about Korea. Only two of my classmates from dental hygiene school knew we married. After Fred's parents died, we finally told lots of people that we had eloped, including family members. We found out his Aunt Gladys and Uncle Bill had done the same thing many years earlier.

The Korean War came to an end and Fred was transferred to Texas. What a relief to find out he didn't have to go war. We planned a public November wedding so I could go to Texas to live with Fred. Both the Arnolds and the Bowmans offered to finance the wedding but I chose the Bowmans as I wasn't going to be beholden to Fred's parents after our disastrous first meeting. I only said yes to Bowmans because I was so angry at Fred's father. Fred didn't care where we got married. HE just wanted me to move to Texas so we could be together. The Bowmans felt our formal wedding was their chance to show what they could afford, so Mrs. Bowman orchestrated the whole affair. When the harpist asked me in what order to play the songs I had picked, I responded, "Ask Mrs. Bowman because I don't know any of the songs—she picked them."

That set an ugly atmosphere for the whole wedding and she didn't speak to me until after the ceremony, when she pinched Fred's cheek so hard that it hurt and said to him, "I hope she will treat you better than she treated me." This confirmed that we made an excellent choice to elope because that earlier wedding was quite wonderful.

Mrs. Bowman told us the president of Bethany's lady committee wanted to see us before we left for our honeymoon. This woman told me how badly I had treated the Bowmans, but her daughter overheard her and told her to stop it because we were looking forward to a honeymoon. She stopped the chiding and said she understood that Mrs. Bowman was too pushy and outspoken. Everyone knew this about her and I'll share a funny aside. When Mrs. Bowman died, the minister couldn't think of anything to say about her and only about a dozen people were at the funeral. This was the story he told. Shortly before she died, she had requested him to ask the funeral home to put underpants on her and when they said they didn't do that, she had him call other funeral parlors to request the underpants. When he found a funeral home that would do as she wanted, Mrs. Bowman had him transfer her funeral to the funeral home where we were sitting. Laughter broke out and I still laugh about her prudishness. That was all he could say about her! During the reception, we all discussed our horror stories about her and everyone had one or more to tell and it made for a fun luncheon.

Now back to my story. The formal wedding was held on November 13, 1954. I must say it was a lovely wedding in her beautifully furnished home with flowers and about 50 guests around a big fireplace. Today we celebrate our anniversary on that date since it was the public affair. But we celebrated our first anniversary in February 1955, so I wasn't thinking about the November date that year. Fred brought me a dozen roses on Nov. 13, which was very unlike him. When I asked why, his mother said indignantly, "Bert, it's your first anniversary." Talk about embarrassment!

We stayed at the Hershey Hotel in Hershey, Pa. for one night so we could be on our way to Wyncote the next morning. Evelyn Ey, the 1954 Miss America, was married that same day and held her reception in the hotel. We were not invited in, but it was exciting to do some people watching.

The next morning we returned to Wyncote to bid Fred's parents goodbye for a year. Fred would be stationed in Texas to finish his time in the service. We were going to live in Texarkana, Arkansas, but both of us worked in Texarkana, Texas. The town was split between two states. I became the first hygienist in Texarkana, and this was before Ross Perot came to town. Fred was to continue ordinance training at the Red River Arsenal. We had to hurry away, as Fred had to be at the base on Monday morning. With tears running down his face, his father kissed Fred on the cheek and bade us goodbye. It stunned me to see his father show emotion. No, he didn't kiss me.

Fred, the watercolorist, today.

The trip to Texas was rushed so Fred wouldn't be AWOL (absent without leave) We stopped only to eat, and thank goodness Texarkana was located at the most northern part of Texas. We drove in Fred's used car, the same Desoto he and his friend used to visit us girls when they were stationed in Aberdeen. That seemed so romantic!

My boss was a fun-loving man about forty years old. We had a lovely, enjoyable working relationship. If we weren't busy, we walked up the hallway from his office to visit two brothers who were both state senators. They were never busy and we often bet on the Hot Springs, Arkansas horse races. I'm not a gambler, but my boss encouraged me to go along and it was fun to join in. I was curious as to why the two senators were never working. When I asked them, they responded," All we have to do is do what the oilmen want." That was my introduction to Texas politics.

My boss's wife would often feed the two of us lunch in their house. I learned to love the delicate taste of okra and enjoyed listening to my boss's childhood stories. We laughed a lot at these luncheons and ate too much. The food was great because my boss's mother-in-law cooked it. His wife didn't like cooking. Life was very different in Texas. The "colored" areas, as they were called at that time were safe to walk through at any hour, and we loved doing that because we heard wonderful music. The residents greeted us if they saw us. Sometimes it was hymns or jazz or current hits, and they were great singers.

We couldn't get the food we could get up north. There were no Jewish delicatessens and I missed many items when I cooked. One day we drove to Dallas to get some of the things I wanted, only to find that they didn't carry anything more than Texarkana. Dallas was a small town back then. One of my friends from dental hygiene school (my maid of honor) was there and we visited her. She was part of the clique at school so it was a pleasurable trip. How different those towns are today.

Fred doesn't read music well and plays the piano by ear, but he did manage to play the bass at dances for officers and noncoms—both "black and white," as they were called in 1954. Segregation still existed in the south so the two dances were held separately. I lost a nice black cleaning lady because she said I didn't know how to treat her. One day I made lunch in the kitchen while she was ironing and offered her a sandwich to have it with me. I offended her, because blacks didn't eat with whites. We were worlds apart culturally, but I didn't know it.

We met two couples that loved jazz as much as we did, and we enjoyed Texas barbeques and music with them. One played the saxophone while Fred played piano. We visited both couples weekly. It was a good year and I was feeling good.

We spent a weekend in New Orleans with Fred's parents halfway through our Texas year and they were relieved to see him happy. They didn't trust that he would be happy with me. I was in a fantasy world full of love and people. It was almost like my dental hygiene student days. Alas, it too had to end.

We were back from New Orleans for less than a month when I cleaned a middle-aged woman's teeth. As I walked across the room, she told me I was pregnant. I was shocked to find she was right. I was disappointed, as I wanted to start a family after we were settled in a home in Pennsylvania and my debt was paid. As I began to accept motherhood, I grew excited and instinctively knew I would have a girl.

We said our goodbyes to all our friends, and I was six months pregnant as we headed back to Wyncote. I knew my life would change in another three months, so I wanted to take a vacation and meander home, but Fred was worried about finding a home for us and getting a job. I felt that could wait, since we would temporarily live with his parents until we could have our own house. It was a miserable trip home. Fred didn't want to make stops or take breaks even if we were hungry or my back ached. This side of Fred was scary to me. He had always been very understanding and lovely with me. I was in tears halfway home.

Back in Wyncote I went into labor and gave birth to a beautiful girl. Patricia was a lactose intolerant baby and couldn't keep any formula down. She regurgitated all day long, even between feedings. I began to feel inadequate and angry, and wondered why my baby didn't like me. It was also obvious that we needed to move out of the Arnolds' home. Fred hated living there. His mother took me house hunting begrudgingly. Finally we found a small Cape Cod style house in a small development in Hatboro, which we could afford but couldn't afford to furnish. It took a year or two to furnish the five rooms. We were broke and we would not go into debt to furnish a house. Many of our neighbors were buying on installments. They saw we had nothing and assumed we were putting money in the bank. We became known as the rich Arnolds in spite of our actual circumstances. Only one other family in our development had any college education.

Four years after Patricia's birth, we had a son, Frederick J. Arnold, Jr. whom we call Dirk. He was a planned baby and I knew I was having a boy and I was right. This was in the days before ultrasound. He was an easier baby than Patricia because he was not lactose intolerant.

I felt totally inadequate in every way. My anger at my situation was almost unbearable. I felt I was in the same mess that my mother was in and she never got out of it. What if I didn't? This was very scary stuff to me. I could snap at Fred at the least infraction. No wonder he became depressed.

One day, at the suggestion of the Bowmans, I visited the president of Bethany's ladies committee, in the hospital. She asked me how much I owed on my college debt. She was empathetic and arranged for her committee to pay one dollar for every dollar I paid. What a relief that was! We lived on Fred's salary while anything I made at dental hygiene went to pay my debt. However, I could only work if Fred was home to babysit because mothers either stayed home in those years or paid a babysitter which we could not afford. Fred's mother would reluctantly babysit if I had a doctor's appointment. She told me that she had babysat her other grandchildren and she was too tired to do it for us. When she did babysit, she would question me about whether I came right from the doctor's office or if I ran errands afterwards. God forbid, if I didn't come straight back to her house. I couldn't afford sitters so I was a 24/7 overwhelmed mother, I was becoming more depressed but, as usual, I was smiling through my problems in front of other people. Fred bore the brunt of my unhappiness and he had no clue about how to help the baby or me. I had no one to talk to and cried a lot. I didn't understand that my childhood feelings were affecting my life. I had already taken care of so many babies at Bethany and two more was overwhelming me. It was almost like the responsibility of caring for all those children had come back to haunt me, but I didn't realize I was revisiting the past.

 I should have talked to a therapist, but we didn't have the money nor did I know about therapists. I was embarrassed to be overwhelmed when other mothers didn't appear to be. Our pediatrician tried his best to help me and was most understanding, but I felt abandoned and alone all over again. Fred couldn't deal with feelings while I wanted to pour them out, so I hid them again. If we could have afforded help of some kind, I might have been a better mom. I felt so desperate and don't know how I lived through this period. My rage was near the surface and at times it was released in unhealthy ways for my children and for Fred. I badly needed support and a mother.

 I worked part time when Fred could babysit, but I hated dental hygiene. My boss was a fundamental Christian and one of his patients "saved" me one day. She said I had to tell my boss, and his response was "Hallelujah." It made me angry that I felt they were trying to control my life. I was thrown by the whole experience because I was afraid to not believe and not sure I was right to disbelieve. They sounded so convincing. I worked this through with our minister, who helped me understand that I didn't have to believe what she told me.

That was when I realized I was an agnostic. I continued to study and read until I was sure that being an agnostic was best for me. That is the spiritual path I still follow today. I believe God gave me a brain and trusts me to use it, and I try to use it to best of my ability. I continued to study with our minister at Beaver College (now known as Acadia College), taking evening courses in religion which he taught. By now our daughter Patricia was four and our parental concerns were not as pressing, but I was still feeling miserable and helpless.

One Friday night Fred came home to tell me he and others were let go from his job drafting industrial furnaces, since he was the only non-engineer. Others were let go because the company was not producing as they once had. After he was unemployed for six months, he was too depressed to even go looking for a job. I had to speak to someone. I tried talking to his mother. Wrong! I told her how I was feeling worried about Fred not looking for a job. She replied, "If you don't want him, we'll take him back." So much for acknowledging or understanding my problems. We were nearly broke, but it was quite clear that Fred's parents wouldn't help us and this took a toll on our marriage and parenting.

Mr. Brown at Brown Brothers and Harriman, the private bank where Fred's father worked, offered Fred a job. Fred's spirits were lifted but not mine were not. I wrongly assumed Fred no longer loved me because of his depression and this added to my problems.

Family parties were hard on me. I said little because I had nothing to say. We didn't have much in common at that time. They talked mostly about business, sports, or their social lives. I couldn't talk about any of those things. I couldn't talk about my insecurities or vulnerabilities. My repertoire was quite small. I was offended very easily in those days, and Fred's family could offend me easily with no awareness that I was hurt. But why would they talk to me when I had nothing to say?

And they didn't know how miserable I was. They all knew about Bethany but weren't interested in my past, so it was never discussed nor did anyone ever go to see Bethany about an hour and a half away. I never told them I wanted them to see it because it was such a great lovely campus. If I told Fred they offended me, he defended them. We fought about this often. His brothers got together socially, but we were often not included. I felt inferior and unwanted. I was alone again and greatly pained, with no one to talk with about my feelings. When I think back, I realize his brothers were six and eight years older than Fred and already successful in their careers, while we were just getting established. One had three children and the other had four, so they were busy with their own problems. I didn't understand this at the time but I can now. I enjoy his surviving brother and his wife when we can get together.

I got a call from a neighbor of my mother-in-law who told me my mother-in-law had a massive heart attack. I had trouble believing it because I had talked to her twice that day about a dress she was making for our daughter. I couldn't believe that she was dead three days later. Our last memory of her was eating her favorite lamb chop dinner. She said to us, "These taste so good," as she smacked her lips. Fred adored his mother and was quite shaken when she died the next day. He had lots of anxiety over her death. After all, the older boys left home to join the service and Fred had many more years alone at home with her. He felt very protective of her because he hated how his father treated her. After her death, Fred fell apart. He couldn't get home from the office without calling me every few minutes along the way. His anxieties were full blown. I talked him into the elevator and onto the train. Once he got to Wyncote, Patricia, Dirk, and I met him and he was fine.

This behavior went on for a month, when I finally suggested he see a psychiatrist. He did so for a year and was able to dispel his depression and anxiety. We never told the family. I was an ace for him but couldn't help myself. I thought no one else in the extended family had problems, so I was the odd ball. I was still looking for a large extended family and could not understand that the three of us were family Somehow, it wasn't enough. I didn't feel that I had a real family who cared about me. I became bitter that I was the only one in the world who felt so defeated.

My children were six and two when I was thirty-two. I know they suffered from my inability to be the mother I wanted to be. I barely managed to do more than tend to their physical needs. I could never understand what it was like to have parents or how parents raised their children, so I tried to have them conform as I had at Bethany. When they did their own thing, I didn't understand and felt unloved by them. I loved them and wanted so much for them to love me. But if my mother never loved me, why would my children? I felt they were lucky to have parents, so why would they cry or give me a hard time by getting angry at me when I issued orders? Every negative response on their part meant to me that I was unloved and inadequate. My upbringing made it impossible to understand normal childhood behavior and to accept it without personalizing everything. I simply had no idea what normal parenting was. I also had too much pride to tell anyone how inadequate I felt. I wanted more from my children than any child can give a parent. I wanted them to understand me, hear me, and help me. Now I see that I was asking the impossible and how unhealthy that was. I realize they did show love, but I did not recognize it as love. I didn't realize until years later how much my desire for a family combined with my bitterness at never having had one myself growing up caused me to expect too much from my children. I was dumping a lot of responsibility on them and I was unaware of what I was doing.

Crazy as it sounds, we moved back to my father-in-law's house in Wyncote after Fred's mother's death. Who knows why except I felt sorry for Fred's father as he never learned to help around the house and I thought he needed help. He treated me poorly and goaded me, as he had done with his wife. Fred was unhappy about his dad's relationship with me, but said it was not new behavior. Instead of fighting back like his wife did, I prepared dinner for the family. When he came in the front door from work, I went out the back door and didn't come home until it was time for the kids to go to bed. I went to a neighbor's house or to a movie or shopping. Fred and I went to our room for the night. There was little interaction between my father-in-law and anyone in our little family of four. I can't remember Dad playing with our children. He came home from work and after dinner sat in the living room smoking his pipe and did not want to be disturbed. Our son was two and our daughter six. How hard this was for them! I thought it was better for me to disappear than for them to listen to the bickering that went on if Fred's father and I were in the same room. Fred kept quiet because, as he told me years before, "No one talks up to my dad."

Financially, we barely existed, as Fred's father charged us room and board and let his maid go, so I could go do the house work in his big three storied house. After working so hard at Bethany for years, this was an added humiliation for me. We were unable to pay our debt, save, or socialize. Our Hatboro house was not selling, so we rented it out temporarily and the renters were a mess. It was overwhelming to manage both homes which were twenty minutes apart, plus parenting two children without support. Fred tried to be supportive but wouldn't stand up to his father. Nor did he understand me or my desperation. The whole situation was a disaster for our family, so I began to look for a house. I told Fred I was moving with him or without him, and he chose unequivocally to come with us. When I told my father-in-law we were moving, he said, "You should go." I replied, "No, we're all going." He was aghast. The shock on his face was amazing to see. He expected me to go alone!

Six months later we bought a house about two blocks from my father-in-law's because we were able to sell our Hatboro house. But I was getting angrier and angrier about my life because it didn't feel better. Fred was providing financial but no emotional support. As usual, I wasn't expressing how I felt because I knew I wouldn't be heard. All my life I had not expected to be seen or heard, and I hadn't learned how to deal with it. Fred knew I was miserable, but couldn't fathom what to do to help. He felt helpless himself and thought I was too sensitive. Our conversations went nowhere. When we were newlyweds, he told me one of the things he loved about me was I was so directed and independent. Neither of us knew that I was as emotionally dependent as he was.

We moved close to my father-in-law so our daughter didn't have to change schools and Fred's father could visit his grandchildren. Our son visited him every weekend for breakfast until he could no longer eat soft-boiled eggs with pieces of shell in them. Dad never came to our house except the day before Christmas (my birthday which he never acknowledged), so he barely saw our children. A neighbor of his informed me that he told her I didn't allow him visits. I explained to her that he could visit at any time, just as our children could visit him any time. With Fred's approval, I wrote to dad explaining visits were fine and saying I was sorry he had told his neighbor a different story. Fred read the letter, approved it, and delivered it. Dad misinterpreted what I said and told Fred that I had written such a terrible letter. Thank goodness I had Fred approve it and Fred defended me. At this time, they were riding the same train to work so Fred saw his father five days a week. They did not sit together because dad wanted to read his paper and so did Fred. They did acknowledge each other each day. Dad still didn't visit except at Christmas time, when he dropped by to see Fred, but he never left a card or gift for our children or for us. I would remain upstairs until he left. I have no idea why he treated our children this way, because if they accidentally met in town he was sociable and pleasant with them. I understood he didn't like me but how can you not see your grandchildren? Mine are so precious to me. Ultimately, I think he actually learned to like my standing up to him, but that took years.

When I was having a difficult time with our teenage daughter in the 1960s, Fred's father would see her from time to time because he felt I didn't love her. He and I had no understanding of each other. He felt I wasn't worthy of his son. Because he had attained upper mobility, he felt marrying an orphan had pulled Fred down. One time he offered our daughter money which was a first for him. She turned it down and called me on the phone to tell me she knew he did it because he thought I didn't care for her so she could not accept it. I loved that she understood the situation and that she shared the story with me.

To compensate for our children not having extended family, we became a host family for foreign students every year. We had students from Saudi Arabia, Hong Kong, Africa, and Taiwan. I enjoyed their visits and felt happy when they were with us. The Saudis, who visited with us for two years, loved our children and played with them often. One was our daughter's friend and the other was our son's. They came for holidays and almost every Saturday night. I can still see them walking through the woods together with our kids sitting around their necks. What great guys they were.

Leaving my father-in-law's home was such a relief for us. Wyncote today is ethnically and religiously mixed, but at that time it was a white protestant town and many people were biased against Catholics, Jews, and blacks. My dear Catholic friend's home, bordered on my father-in-law's property. They asked me to ask dad if he would sell his house to them and he said no. He told us, if Catholics moved in, Jews would follow and then blacks. This is exactly what has happened and it is still the nice community it always was.

Chapter Twelve

WE MOVED TO A lovely old stone duplex in Wyncote. I was so depressed that I could barely function, but I continued to put one foot in front of the other. I was not emotionally available for our children. My body was there, but my soul and mind were numb. I could still perform in a perfunctory way, but I was at the end of my rope. Fred didn't understand. Our marriage was in trouble, but I was too distraught to think about it. I wanted to fall into a pit and cover myself until I could die.

What I didn't understand at this time was the effect of my past on the present. Since I felt unloved and unlovable, I acted in a way at home that made me unlovable. I was unconsciously fighting Fred and the children to prove to myself that I was unlovable. He fought back with nasty language, which only added fuel to the fire. We were beginning to disrespect each other, and pull further and further away.

I hoped a therapist could help me divorce. I know now that would not have been the answer. We actually loved each other despite our problems. Everyone who knew us always told me how much Fred adored me. It showed on his face, but I could neither see it nor trust it. No one had ever loved me, so why would I trust that Fred did?

I was teaching Sunday school as a non-believer, so my children would have an idea of their birth religion. I taught Patricia's confirmation class and the last assignment I gave them was to write a letter to the minister and tell him why they wanted to join the church. I got a call from the minister who told me we had a problem. Her letter told him why she didn't want to join the church. I laughed and said that was no problem because if she felt that way, she shouldn't join. He was so relieved because he thought I was going to be so upset.

I thought I would meet happy people in the congregation but that didn't materialize. I did make friends, but no one close enough to confide in. So I continued to smile any time I was in other people's company. At that time, the church the Arnolds attended was the center of our community's social activity. To get out of the house, I started to volunteer in the church's kitchen for church affairs. I tried to become engaged in order to forget my problems at home, but it didn't work.

Finally, I made the decision to go into therapy. I was in my mid-thirties and it was time to clear my head. I started with a psychologist, Dr. Leckerman, who was very nice and did a good job, but because I had a serious problem with intimacy, I quit going when I should have stayed. Then I went to a psychiatrist to work on my anger and I began to take it out on him. He could be as sharp with words as Fred's father, so I became quite feisty with him. In his defense, he told me abandonment issues are the hardest to work through. He was conducting psychoanalysis, and I knew he didn't always listen to me because I would digress just to see if he was asleep. He often closed his eyes. Sometimes he didn't know what I said, and since I had never been heard as a child, I could barely tolerate his inattentiveness. It was helpful when he explained that I had PTSD (post-traumatic stress disorder). I did work hard to overcome that part of my traumas.

After two years I suggested we terminate. By that time I felt a little better and he had done all he could for me. He set a date because he agreed it was time to quit. That made it easier for me to leave, as I was emotionally attached to him so it left me feeling abandoned again.

Another psychiatrist was recommended to me and I started to go to him three times a week. One night when I was having an extremely hard time, I called him up and told him what was going on with me and that I couldn't deal with it. It was a Friday. He told me to come to his office. When I got there, he bawled me out for interrupting his wife's birthday party. I said, "I didn't ask to come. You told me to come." With that he gave me a hard hit. He hit me so hard that I flew onto his sofa across the room and hit my head against the wall. I feared abandonment so intensely, I kept seeing him and it never entered my mind to report him. I told him that if he ever abused me again, I would walk out for good. About a year after that incident he screamed at me about some minor thing I can't remember. I stood up and walked out for good. He had the audacity to bill me for the session, which I didn't pay. Then I got a bill the following week when I didn't show, but that also remained unpaid. I was learning to trust and respect myself. The emptiness was gone and I was finally a person.

Fred and I began to work with Dr. Martin Goldberg, a wonderful family and marriage psychiatrist. Dr. Goldberg was extremely caring and gentle and worked through our problems with us. My personal issues were now subsiding but they were not yet fully resolved and I guess no one totally resolves them. I felt I had to continue my therapy until completion. I was reading about Transactional Analysis at this point and was taking lessons in that modality. I will come back to this later on.

I threw out my dental hygiene uniform after work one evening and told Fred I was going to attend social work school at Temple. I believed it was a means for me to improve my life and prepare me for a career that I could also use as a coping mechanism. My son was unhappy coming home to an empty house. I could see how hurt he felt, but social work school was such an oasis that I kept it my priority despite the guilt I felt. My intent was not to hurt my son, but to do something that might give me relief from myself. Our son was a sensitive child and I still feel guilty for the things I did that hurt him.

At Bethany, we fell in line when orders were issued, so when our daughter rebelled I didn't know how to cope. I was a conscientious student and could repress my feelings and be happy at school. I managed through the downs to become an honor student. I dreaded coming home to an unhappy family. Fred had no sisters, so he didn't understand our daughter and neither were we able to help each other.

I was in my thirties when we finally paid off my college debt. We celebrated with a party and my father-in-law attended. I told him why we were having the party and he never said a word not even congratulations. I wanted so much for a compliment from him to hear that I was now acceptable, but nothing was said. That hurt. Fred was now able to support us well and we were fighting less. I was still not happy, but the depression was gone. Thank goodness it has not returned since.

During the 1960s, family and national values were being challenged. A minister at our church taught classes revolving around national politics and family issues. When no one in the class admitted to problems, I believed only I had them. I had no clue about how to attain what I assumed was the joy and contentment they experienced in their families. The minister and his wife invited us to their home many times. We laughed a lot and played games after dinner. Eventually, they decided to divorce and in retrospect I know he was a womanizer. He was empathic and fun and a great listener, and attempted to help me. He was also teaching the new psychotherapy of Transactional Analysis (TA). Everyone was reading the book *I'm OK, You're OK*, considered the bible for TA. We began to plan lessons and teach it together. I also began to teach on my own at the local library.

After the divorce, he moved to Michigan. I missed his attention and compliments. He held therapy groups every night at an institute in Bloomfield, Michigan using TA, and asked me to join him as his co-therapist. This was during the 1960's when it felt like the world was going mad in seeking liberation from old values.

I left Fred and my children the day before Nixon's 1972 November reelection. In a week I knew my rosy opinion of the minister was inaccurate, but I was too proud to admit my error. He was a good listener and complimentary, but only in his work. Our son came to see me twice to request that I come home, which I did on January 2, 1973. The two months away from home felt like years. I spoke with both Fred and Dirk often on the phone. I still loved Fred, and he thought we could work through our problems if we were together. I still regret the scars this separation caused our family.

Psychoanalysis didn't work well for me, although both therapists helped me to some degree. I found the silences almost unbearable. Maybe it would have worked with different psychiatrists who were more sensitive to the depths of my neurosis. I also admit I was a tough client, with much damage to my psyche. TA made me feel heard, as the therapist did more talking. I appreciated their direct responses and interactions with me.

One problem I was working through was the need to distance myself from people. I came to understand that I could give up my search for family because my husband and children were my family. Believe it or not, that was a huge learning experience for me. I also learned I could accept or reject Fred's family of origin. I was encouraged to avoid family affairs. That was a choice I made and have since regretted it. I feel the therapist was wrong to tell me this. Although I told Fred it was okay to go to family affairs without me, he did not want to go unless I accompanied him. After that visits with any of the family only occurred if mother was hosting a holiday. Before her death, we did occasionally entertain my in-laws or they had us for dinner. We no longer received invitations from family. Fred's two brothers and their seven children would get together with their father, but we were not included. I regret not knowing my nieces and nephews better, although I do know some of them today and am thankful for that.

The therapist and I discussed the disdain I had for my name because of the unloving manner in which it was given to me. He helped me understand that I could legally change it to any name I wanted. I chose Bert, as my friends already called me that and I wanted them to name me. The chauvinist judge honored my request if I would cook a nice dinner for my husband that night. My lawyer, a friend, warned me to hold my tongue, so I responded by saying we were going out to dinner that night to celebrate, but that I would cook the following night. My request was granted. I no longer respond to any communications addressed to my old name, nor to people who call me by my old name. I detest the old unloving ugly one.

I had to work through all the negativity that surrounded me and I felt I was drowning in negative attitudes and experiences. Negativity was what pulled me down to a point I could barely survive. I feel now as if I cannot tolerate such negativity any more. If I encounter negativity, I refuse to participate. I walk away because it brings back all the pain I once felt and no longer want in my life.

Dr. Leckerman and Dr. Goldberg were very helpful to Fred and me. After being in and out of therapy for twenty years, in 1982, at age 52, I finally felt free and ready to face the world and have not felt the need to continue therapy. Except for the usual disagreements, Fred and I do well together. We learned not to escalate arguments and how to resolve them. I have many of the same neuroses, but I have learned to recognize and analyze them until I work through them. I used to get cranky and my neurosis would take over when we went left our house for vacations. Leaving my house even temporarily made me feel homeless. With or without our children, it felt awful but I now know that my home is within me and I can take it anywhere and be comfortable. My feelings of inadequacy and abandonment no longer rule my life. When they rear their ugly heads, I work through them and move on. I have learned to like socializing and enjoy people immensely. Dr. Goldberg once told me that I trust people too much. I think I have overcome that too so I pick and choose friends carefully.

On Christmas Eve in 1984, a neighbor called to inform us that my father-in-law was roaming Wyncote's largest street looking for his coat. We went to his house to find him confused and in bed. Fred's brother placed him in a nursing home the next day because his mind had begun to fade. About ten months later, when it became apparent that he was close to death and frightened, he held my hand as he pleaded with me: "Help me to survive. Please help me to survive." When I explained why I couldn't do that, his look was one of understanding but I'm not sure he accepted the inevitable.

As a trained social worker, I helped him through the death and dying process at his own pace. He would start out by telling me that he was walking down a long hall and wanted me to walk with him. I promised I would go as far as the door but he would have to go in alone with Ruth (his wife) on the other side waiting for him. He believed in heaven so he relaxed. Events occurred on our way which seemed to be events he wanted to resolve and I think we did resolve them. He would continue the process each time I visited, despite his dementia. He assured me he had not cut me out of his will. I suppose he thought money was my major concern, as it was for him. I responded by telling him, "I never did give a damn about your money or I wouldn't have fought with you." This shocked and amazed him. Death was near and he could barely speak because of congestive heart failure, but as Fred held his hand he whispered, "I love you." It was the first time Fred had ever heard those words from his father. We went home that night expecting to see him the next morning. The nursing home promised to call if death was imminent but they did not. The next morning Fred's brother called to say their father had died.

In the mid-1960s I began visiting my mother almost weekly in her subsidized housing. I had not talked to her since I left Bethany almost twenty years before. I wanted to know her feelings about my father and how she dealt with losing her children. What did she know about our lives at Bethany? Had she heard me sing on the radio? How did she feel about my sister Pearl? She was always adverse to Pearl and I had no idea why and still don't.

One weekend Fred invited her to visit us. We drove her from Reading to our house although she was so nervous she vomited most of the way to our house, however, I believe she enjoyed the weekend. We played a game together called I DOUBT IT. You lie about what cards you have in the game until someone says, "I doubt it." If you are caught lying, you lose. She could not lie. We urged her over and over again that lying was part of the game, but she couldn't do it. This was my first glimmer of positive feelings for her. Maybe she was a nice lady after all. Maybe it was hard to see a family having a fun game together.

My mother's life had been so painful that she could not delve into the past. Although she told me the story of how I had been named, I learned little else from her.

She claimed to have forgotten about my father and our removal from her. I believe she probably had because she was so beaten down and depressed. Perhaps forgetting was her means of survival or she couldn't talk about it because her own pain was too painful. On our last visit, she pointed to her TV and said, "I used to love watching it. Now I look at it and think about what I should have done with my life versus what I did." She wanted so much more out of life but didn't know how to make good things happen. That was such a harsh, hard punishment for her, I ceased my questioning. She needed no more pain. I never saw her again except at her funeral.

Thirty years later, in 1994, my brother informed me that our mother was sick in the hospital and would not live much longer. He asked if I wanted to see her. I told him no and never visited her. I pitied her, but I still was not aware of her true self and I didn't want to relate to an empty shell. Now, I am sorry I didn't go because maybe on her death bed we might have talked. I regret that I bought in to the matrons at Bethany who bad mouthed her. She was a victim of herself and her family. She died soon after I got the call and she was 86 years of age. At the funeral I asked the minister, "What do you say about a woman who accomplished nothing in her life?" He replied, "She had you, didn't she?" A burden was lifted from my shoulders. She gave me the tremendous gift of life, and who could not love the person who gave you that gift?

My fear of her having a pauper's grave was assuaged. She somehow managed to save money for an upper middle class funeral. She must have saved all her life for this event and probably would have been happy about how it turned out. The coffin was open and Pearl had bought her a lovely gown in spite of our mother's dislike for her. Pearl was so proud of what she had done as she pointed it out to me. Too bad our mother could not appreciate the longing Pearl had for her and for her approval. There were about twenty cars (all family) in a procession to the gravesite, located at the base of a lovely hill on the outskirts of Reading. Most of her children were there. She had picked and paid for it herself. Finally, in death, she got what she wanted!

During my career as a social worker, I became Director of Social Services at the Montgomery County Emergency Unit of Norristown State Hospital. I moved on to become a social worker at Philadelphia General Hospital, a training hospital for psychiatrists. I learned so much from two psychiatrists there. During the Vietnam Conflict, as a Red Cross volunteer, it was impressed upon us that the country had not declared war. It was a conflict. I worked as a volunteer at the Philadelphia Naval Hospital, designing and running a group to help Vietnam amputees return to civilian life. When the conflict ended, I left to earn a Master's degree in social work and to earn my Academy of Certified Social Workers (licensing) certification. I continued Transactional Analysis training and practice. I attended many psychoanalysis training programs at the Institute of Pennsylvania, and took weeklong summer training courses at Yale, Cornell, and other places. During this period I heard Margaret Mead lecture at the Jewish Y in Philadelphia. Six of us took her to lunch and it was a thrill to listen to her in such an intimate setting. I also was asked to take Virginia Satir to lunch with the same six ladies. She was fun. I forget if she was a psychologist or psychiatrist but I do remember she was a hoot.

Burned out from working with the mentally ill, I became supervisor of four group homes run by the Methodist Home for Children, a residential program for children. They were the worst kids I ever knew re drugs, behavior at home and at school and I loved them all. In 1985 I retired at age 55. I volunteered at an adoption center, United Way, and spent ten years on Bethany's board of directors. I left the board when I realized most members had no interest in making changes, such as providing psychiatric help for the children. The superintendent was a minister and the board was comprised of mostly ministers. They wanted to hear nothing but good things about Bethany and ignored any comment they deemed negative about Bethany's program. I couldn't bear traveling over an hour to hear board members talk about the stock market and have a banker on the board give the members tips for their personal investing. They wanted to hear that Bethany had a perfect program and believed it. They refused to take anything

I said as fact, and didn't investigate what I had found to be legitimate complaints. For ten years I also served on the board of Montgomery County Children and, one of my sources for learning about Bethany's shortcomings. I was on the board of the Wilma Theater, where I still attend performances when I can. I feel it is still Philadelphia's finest theater. My volunteer work was very gratifying and I'm proud of what I accomplished.

Fred and I moved to Ocean City, N.J. for a fourteen-year period. Fred grew up at the shore in the summer and was excited about moving back. He became successful as a watercolorist and loved the shore, but I wanted to be closer to my children and grandchildren, and that was the major impetus to move back to Pennsylvania about fourteen years later. Life was empty for me in New Jersey. There were many cliques, like in most small towns, and as an agnostic I felt like a misfit in a fundamental Christian community. We moved to a suburb, Upper Gwynedd.

Life is a happy, busy journey for us at 84. Fred and I are living in a 55+ community and are happy together. We have our differences, but enjoy our lives. We have a lot in common, such as jazz, reading, the gym, family, and more. He loves that I cook almost every night and doesn't object to cleaning up after dinner. That is a real joy for me. He plays tennis and piano, and is a great watercolorist. I continue to take college courses in history or geography. If only I could tell Mr. Stoltzfus that he fostered those interests in me. I go to the gym every day and get all kinds of positive comments about my walking the treadmill for an hour at the age of eighty four. I even like myself and appreciate how much work it took to be able to say that. I don't strive for perfection but I do continue to try to grow.

Fred and I have achieved our goal of happiness and have enjoyed our lives together these last thirty years. Not only are my depression and emptiness gone, but so is any bitterness I felt. We celebrated our 60th anniversary this year and our rough years were worth the effort. We worked hard to get here.

We have traveled all seven continents and hope to continue exploring new places for years to come. We sometimes take our grandchildren with us. They seem to enjoy each trip and we feel flattered that they travel with their old grandparents. Our children and grandchildren take precedence over everything. Two grandchildren live in Philadelphia's center city, so lunch with them is a marvelous treat and I indulge often. I am unhappy only when my children or grandchildren are unhappy. I want happiness for all of them.

I no longer regret my life because it was what it was and I feel I have survived, grown, and learned how to live. I know no one ever truly gets over all the abandonment issues, but if you have the courage to look at your traumas and work hard to overcome their effects, you can begin to live fully. All the support I got at Bethany contributed greatly to my recovery because I could not have done it. My mother could not have given me what Bethany, Miss Anna, and Mr. Stoltzfus gave me. Mr. Stoltzfus and Miss Anna kept my spirit alive by believing in me and caring for me. I probably would never have found loving people like them if I had stayed home with my mother. They kept the light within me burning and helped me not to extinguish it. They taught me to face hardships until they were resolved. Bethany was a better institution than most of that era, and I understand and accept its shortcomings. I sincerely believe they did the best they could do which is all we can expect even from parents. It was definitely better than what Bethany offers children now. When we were placed, there were no federal programs. The church sent us to Bethany. Foster homes or adoptions were not the *modus operandi* at that time. We could make Bethany home as we were not moved around from placement to placement. How children survive multiple placements is beyond me. Many are returned home when home is not a good place for their growth. Institutions are thought of as a last resort today. It is the quality of the institution that is bad and not the concept of institutionalization. Today's system leaves so much to be desired that it is frightening to think what it must be like to rely on a system that is so broken. No child at Bethany ever died of abuse. It happens too often today in children's placements. How lucky I was to go there and to be befriended by two staff members who truly were parents to me. Workers today must realize that the negativity I spoke about earlier is so ubiquitous that anything that is not positive for placed children, is so deeply felt that the pain it causes is barely describable.

My children, grandchildren, and friends love me as I love them. I feel my past is just that—the past. Without that past, I don't think I would have achieved what I have achieved. Being open to changing one's life is a gift, and I worked so hard in therapy to change and hope I always continue that process. It took a long time, but little by little I was able to see my problems and face them. I still have many of the same neuroses (don't we all?) but they are manageable. I hope to have many more years of peace and contentment. I still get caught up in negative feelings, but then I settle down and think. This process of working through the negativity can be short or last for days, but I stick with working through them until I feel positive. I catch myself living in my inner world from time to time and talk to myself to get myself out into the bigger world. I want to be sharing with the people I feel are my positive kindred spirits and friends.

I'm no longer so outspoken, but I try to be honest without being hurtful. Before therapy, I was often not aware of how my words could be hurtful to others so now I choose my words carefully. I accept when I'm wrong and try to right it. I've learned that I alone make my own neuroses. The beauty of this realization is that if you own them yourself, you can also fix them. If you continually blame others for your problems, you can't work through them. You're off the hook. And you sure can't change the other guy. My family knows that I don't always succeed at this, but I accept that I can't be perfect.

I walk away from negativity and dismiss it from my life as I don't want it to bring me down. Family must smile in photographs before I will display them.

Even the therapist who abused me was helpful. When I talked about my fears of becoming like my mother and told him, "The apple doesn't fall far from the tree," his response was, "Unless the tree is on a hill." That made me realize that parents do not determine who you become. Only you can do that.

Before therapy I kept my emotions to myself. I know how much that harmed me and now I express them. I wish I could have expressed these feelings to my children when they were young, but at the time I did the best I could. I love my life as I am living it, and plan on many more years with Fred and family. No, I do not have my mother's baggage but I still have my own. Yes, I am happy. The beauty of therapy was that it removed all denial and forced me to look at myself. Facing your demons is the only route to having a full life. Life is what we make it, and I want to make it as positive as I can. Deep down in me there was always that glimmer of hope and optimism. I was right when I looked out the window and thought, "Somewhere out there it can be better."

Acknowledgements

WRITING THIS BOOK HAS been emotionally tough but very cathartic, because the demons were quieted with my perseverance. At times I had to put the writing aside because the pain would take over, but this helped me to work through the traumas. It has been a worthwhile endeavor and it has helped me to become more comfortable in my skin. Thank you, everyone, who helped me in this process.

Thank you, Dirk and Patricia, for your love and attention. Dirk did a lot of listening and Patricia is always there for me when I need her.

Thank you, Fred, for all that you contributed to this book. You're editing and drawings have completed my book in a lovely way. Most of all, I thank you for trusting that I would get my life together and never did you complain about the expense of that journey. Through the worst of our problems you stuck by me. I love you for all of that and more. Thank you, too, for loving me as I love you.

I thank my steadfastly loyal grandchildren for loving me despite whatever inadequacies I have shown. You are all dear to me and I love you all. May your journeys be fruitful and may you all be happy. They encouraged me to write until I had a book. They supported me through many crises and helped me through the worst of my times with the book. I love you dearly.

I don't want to forget my lovely ex-daughter-in-law, Donna, who typed my manuscript and spurred me on to keep going. Her computer skills were so helpful. She and my son gave me two wonderful children. Her love for me is as real as mine is for her. Thank you, Donna. You too are one of my kindred spirits.

Thank you, my deceased friend, Ellery French. You accepted me through all my trials, never judged me, and loved me as a friend unconditionally. You had faith in me to get my act together. I loved you, miss you, and will never forget you.

Thank you, Evan and Max, for believing your grandmother could write a book. You also kept me going with your encouragement and love.

Thank you, Dr. Bernard Rice and dear Joan Rice for introducing me to White and for the support you have given me both medically and emotionally. Joan was a dental hygiene student with me so we have a long history. I knew Bob before Bob met Joan. They are also kindred spirits.

Thank you, LeRoy Gensemer, for being a real brother to me and supporting me through all my travails and loving me unconditionally as you did all our siblings.

Thank you, Judith White for your most helpful editing and encouragement while you were writing your third book. Reading your wonderful books spurred me on to keep going. I am looking forward to your third in your series, the first being *The Seventh Etching*. It was a joy to meet you and work with you. What a treat it has been to come to know you.

Thank you Dan Rothman, a Philadelphia lawyer, who edited and was astute about what I needed to do to improve the grammar and punctuation.

Thank you Mary Anne Raimondo for reading the book twice because her first thought was so insightful and enlightening that I had her reread it to be sure I took care of the problem she saw. She was an ace! You are a real joy in my life.

All my therapists had some positive influence even when I felt I had to leave them. Some more than others. Dr. Goldberg kept me working on my marriage. Without him there would have been no Bert and Fred. A nicer, gentler, kind of man would be hard to find.

If I forgot anyone, I apologize. Please let me know if I slighted you.

I hope this book has answered my family's questions about who I am. For social workers who work with children in placements, I hope this book helps illuminate the deep feelings and pain that placement creates. The emotions are so deep you never get past them, but you do learn to live with them. If you have helped one child, you have been a success in your work. The system makes it a challenge to influence a child but you must try. I look forward to many more years with all the people who are so important in my life, and to the remembrances of others who I will always love and carry with me.

www.ingramcontent.com/pod-product-compliance
Lightning Source LLC
Chambersburg PA
CBHW070851050426
42453CB00012B/2145